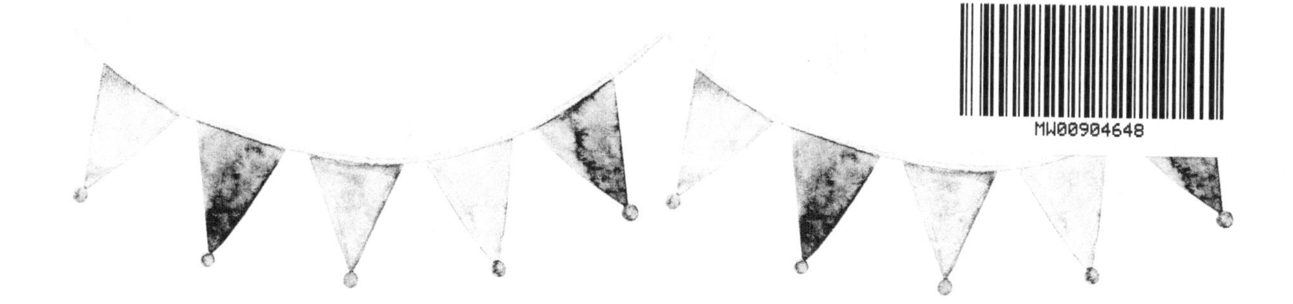

MY FIRST PIANO SONGBOOK

40 Easy Sheet Music

ANYONE CAN PLAY

WITH GAMES + WORKSHEET

Name:______________________________

Date Started:______________________

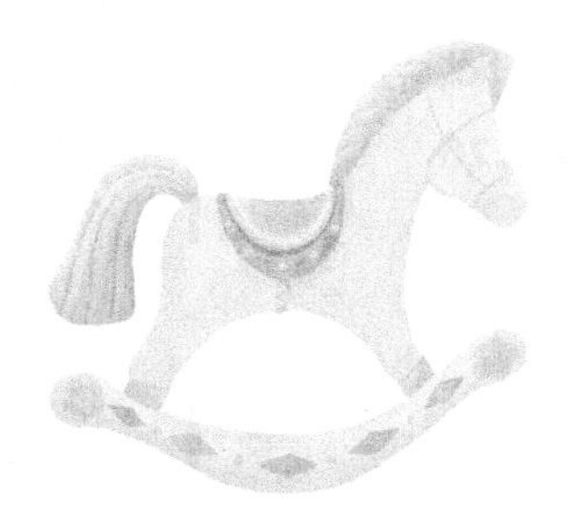

 Published by Lido Publishing

Table Of Content

As you learn each song, color in the mouse to track your progress!

Chapter 1

TOP SECRET

Hey you! Meowzart has misplaced 4 top secret documents throughout the book. Locate all of them and use your musical skill to solved the mystery!

Chapter 2

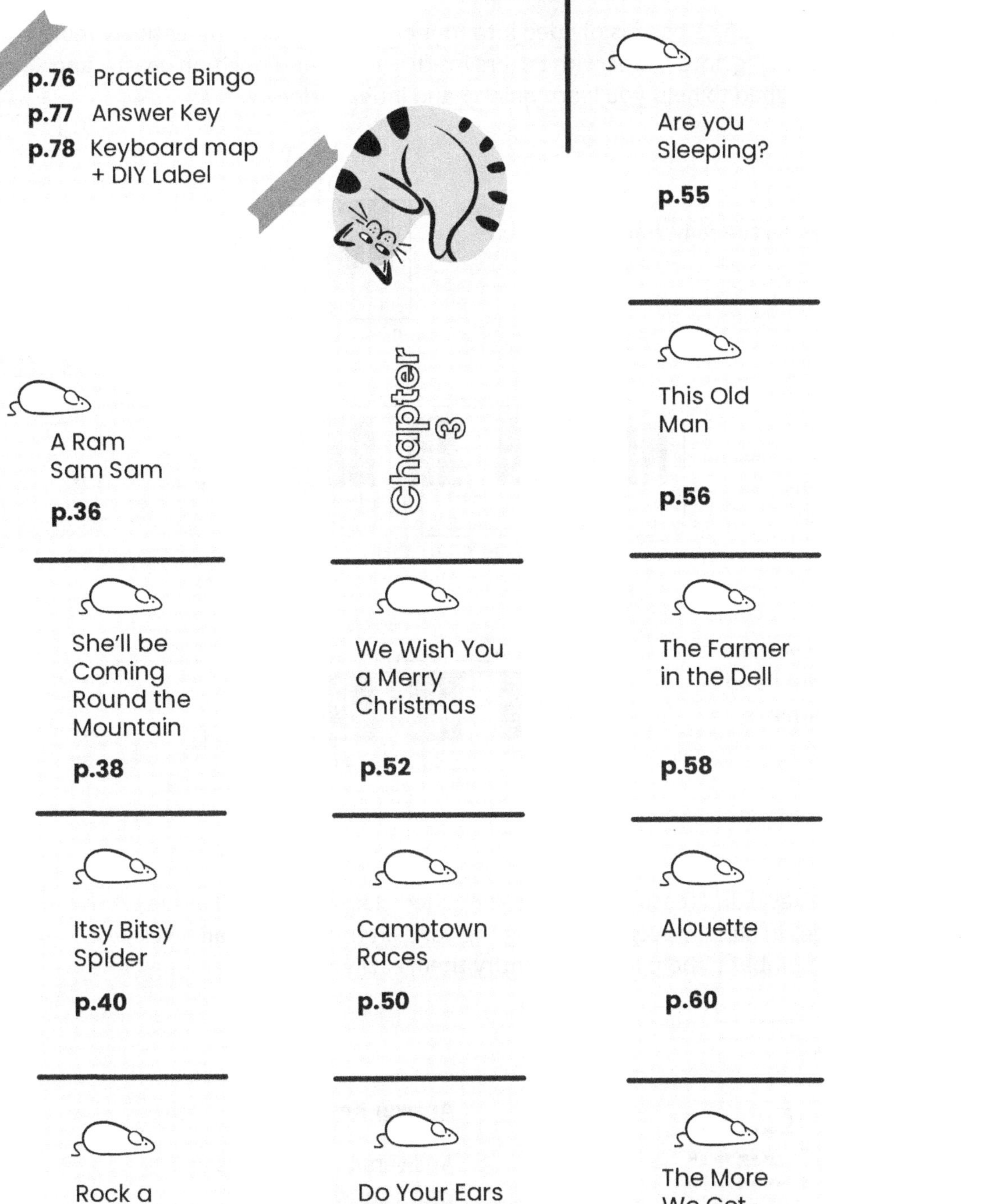

Chapter 3

Chapter 4

Introduction

Welcome to My First Piano Songbook. The book is divided into four chapters, each progressively more challenging. Each song comes with big note heads with letters inside them, hand position charts, and fingering. These features are designed to help you learn quickly and independently.

Chapter 1

All songs in this chapter focuses on the right hand C position.

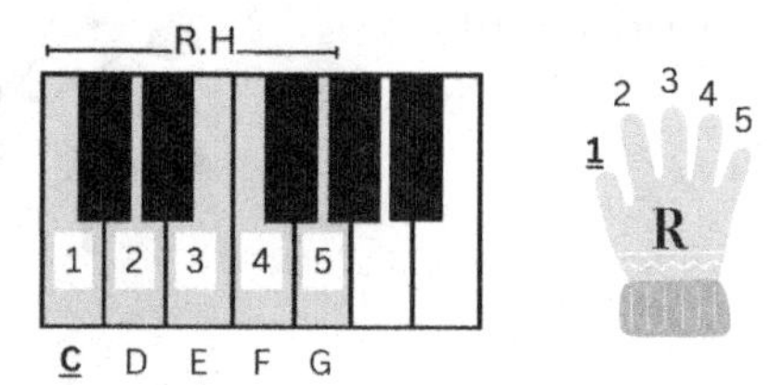

Chapter 2

Introduces playing with both hands together, all songs in this chapter uses the following hand position where the right hand thumb is on middle C.

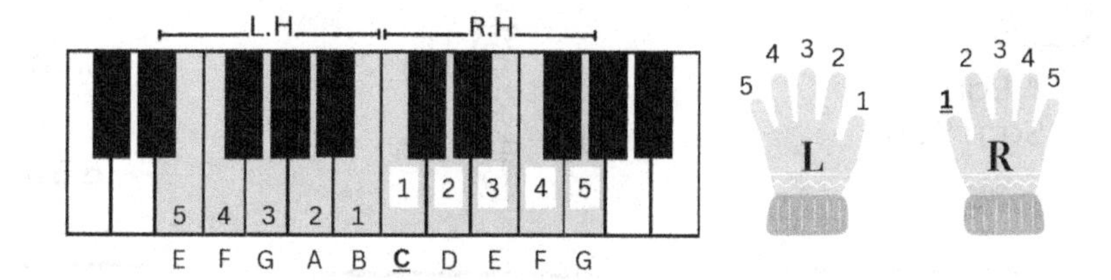

Chapter 3

Continues with playing hands together but introduces a slightly different hand position where the left hand thumb is on middle C.

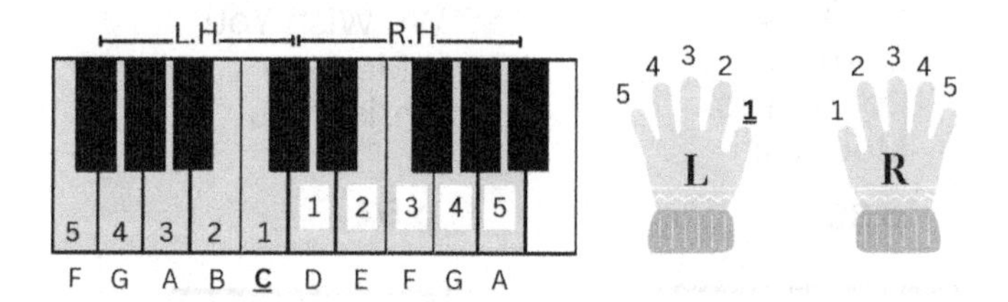

Chapter 4

Includes sharps and flats (black keys) and features a bonus simplified classical song, "Fur Elise." This section introduces small changes in hand movement during the song. In this section, all black keys have a circle around the finger number to help learner identify them easily.

Bonus Features:

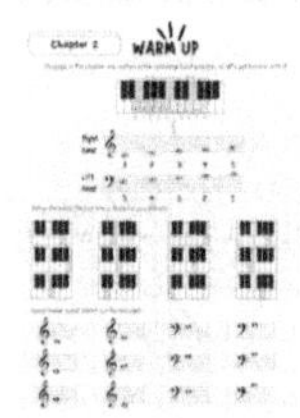

Warm-up Worksheets

Complete the warm-up worksheets before playing the songs in each section. They will help you get familiar with hand positions and notes that you will find in the songs.

Games

There are 4 top secret documents scattered through the book. Use your musical skill to solve the mystery!

Answer Key

Answers to the games and warm-up worksheets questions are in the back of the book on p. 77

Practice Bingo

Turns practice into a game! Fun ideas to practice piano - p.76

Keyboard Map + Label

Helpful reference and make your own keyboard label - p.79

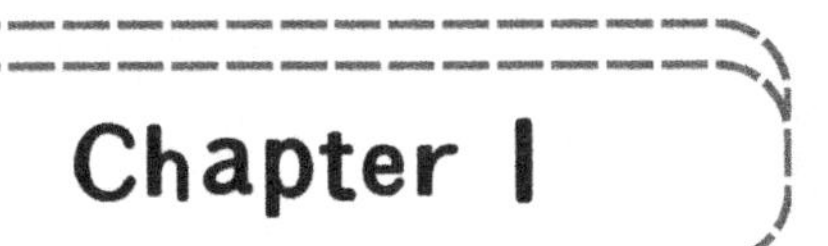

Write the finger numbers for the circled finger inside the box. The first one is done for you!

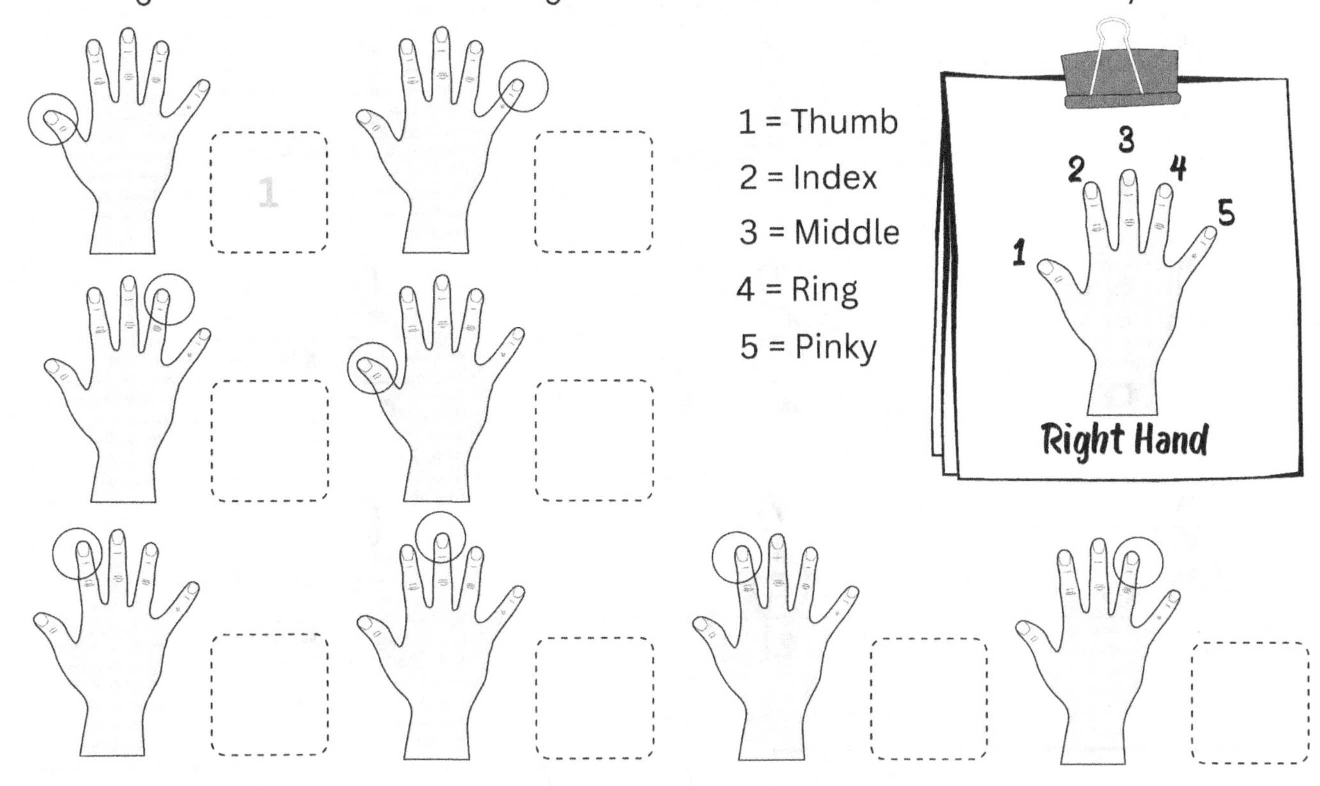

All songs in this chapter are written in the following hand position, so let's get familiar with it!

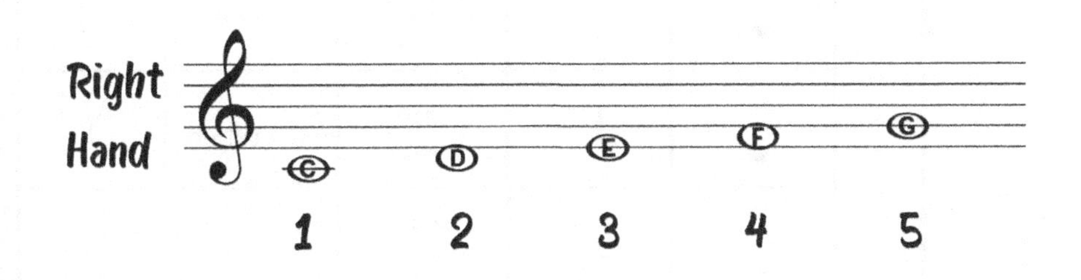

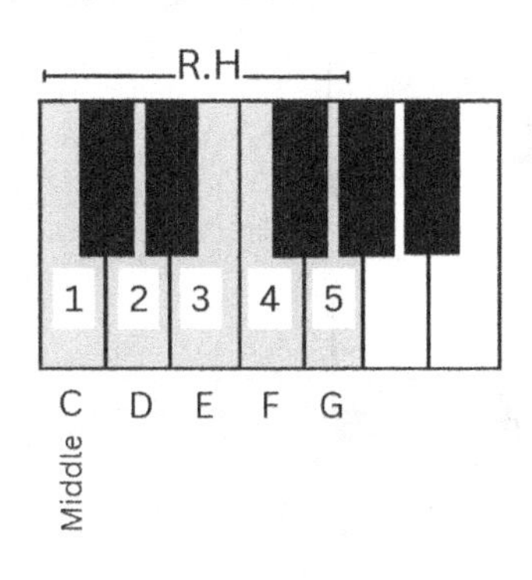

Name the keys! The first one is done for you already.

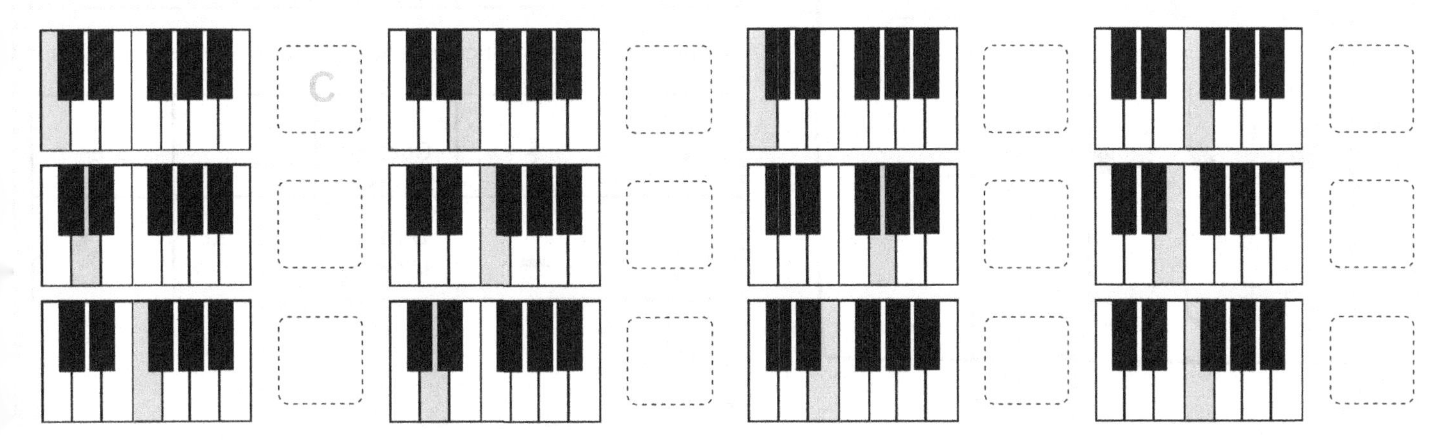

Directions: Name these C position Notes

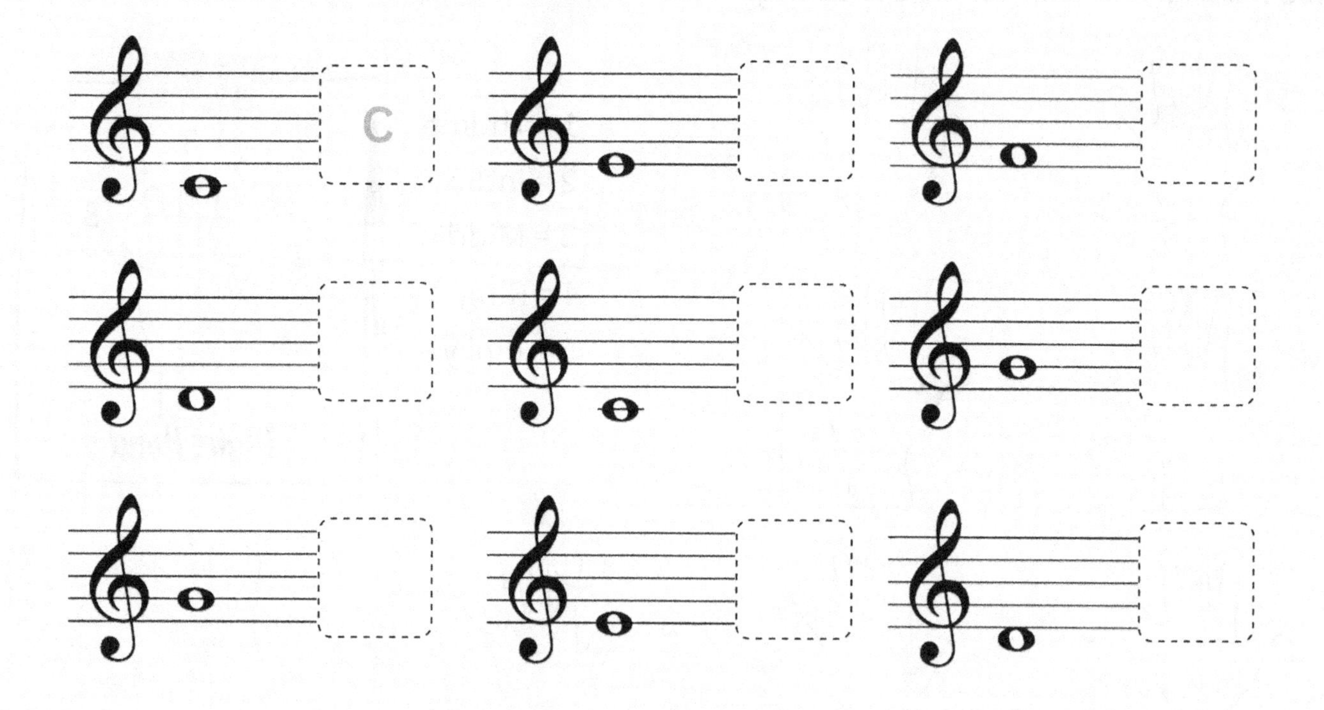

Count the beats to solve the math equations:

𝅝 + 𝅘𝅥 = 5

𝅘𝅥 + 𝅘𝅥 = ______

𝅗𝅥. + 𝅘𝅥 = ______

𝅘𝅥 + 𝅘𝅥 + 𝅘𝅥 = ______

𝅗𝅥 + 𝅗𝅥 + 𝅗𝅥 = ______

Note	Rest	American Name	British Name	Beats in 4/4
𝅘𝅥𝅮	𝄾	Eighth note	Quaver	1/2
𝅘𝅥	𝄽	Quarter note	Crotchet	1
𝅗𝅥	𝄼	Half note	Minim	2
𝅝	𝄻	Whole note	Semibreve	4

"A Dot placed after a note increases its length by half of its original value."

𝅘𝅥.	𝄽.	Dotted Quarter note	Dotted Crotchet	$1\frac{1}{2}$
𝅗𝅥.	𝄼.	Dotted Half note	Dotted Minim	3

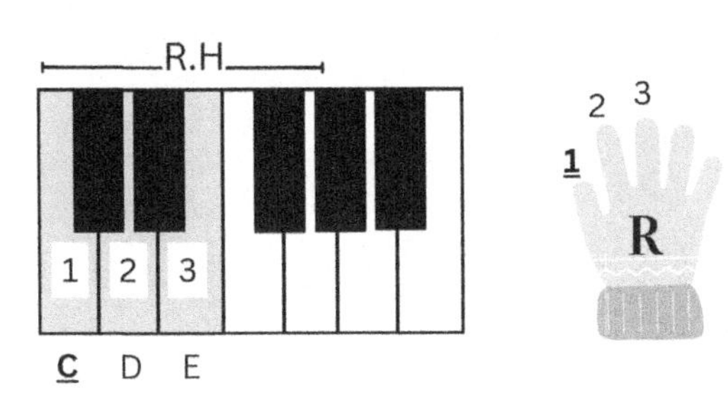

Right hand thumb on middle C

1. Look at the Hand Position Map
2. Find Starting Note
3. Read the Sheet Music
4. Use the Correct Finger Numbers
5. Play Slowly and Count the Beats
6. Increase Speed Gradually

Hot Cross Buns

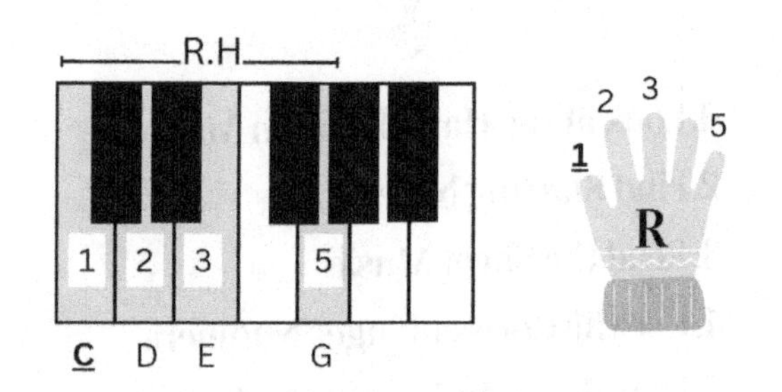

Mary Had a Little Lamb

Lowell Mason

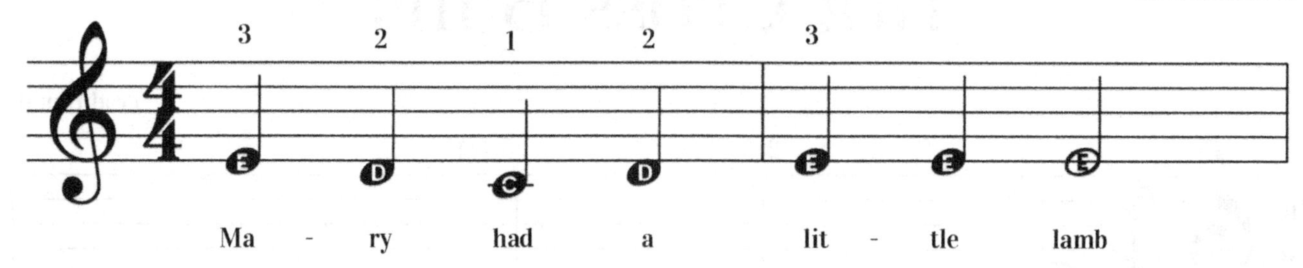

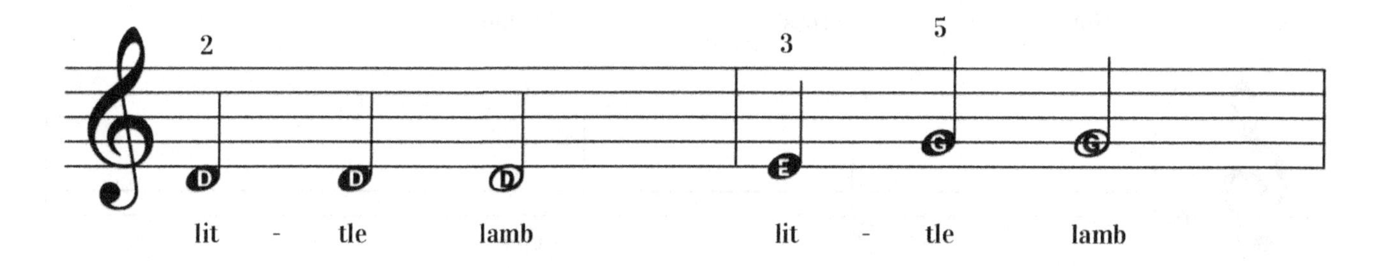

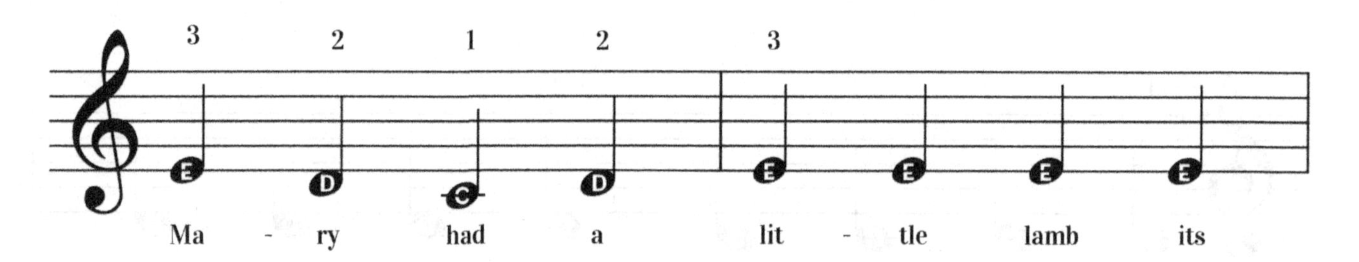

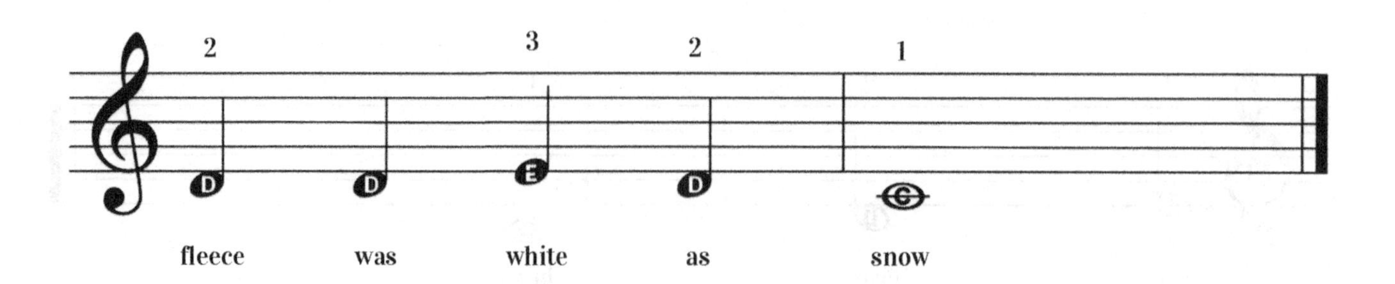

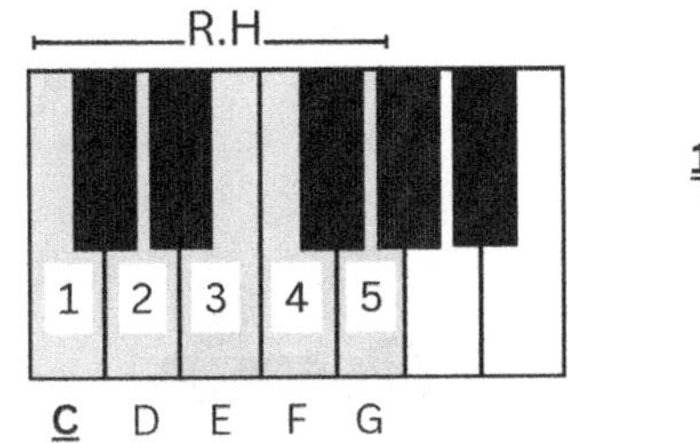

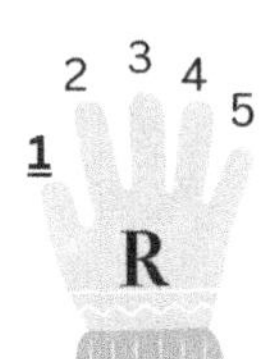

Rain, Rain Go Away

Traditional

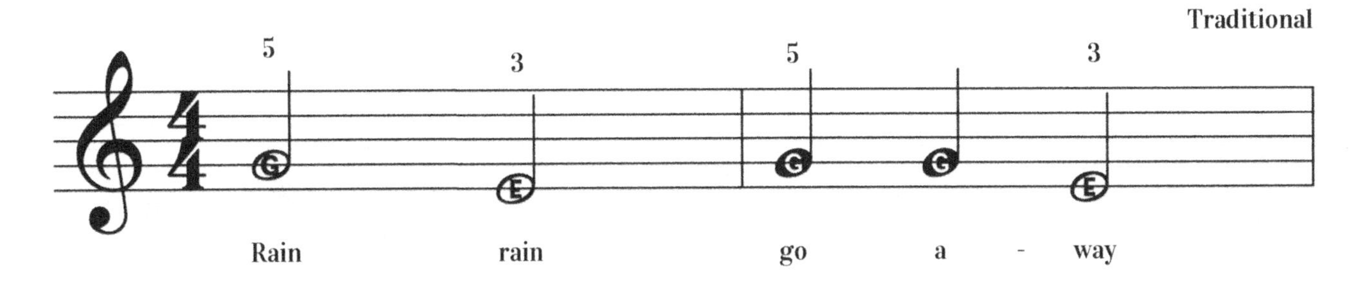

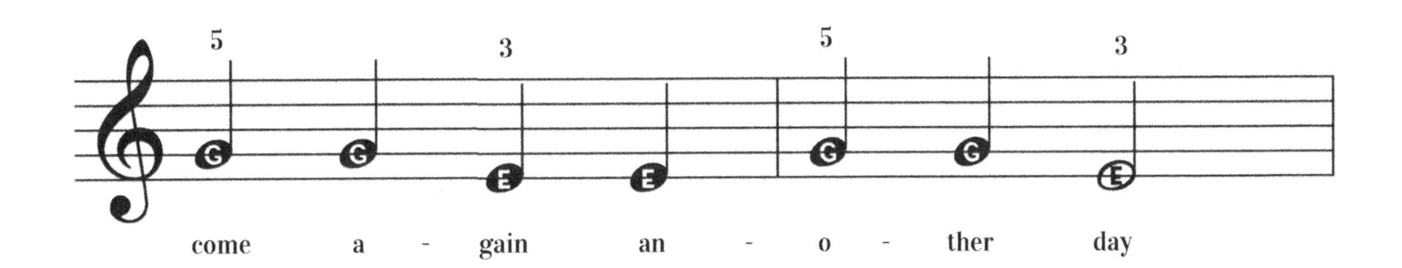

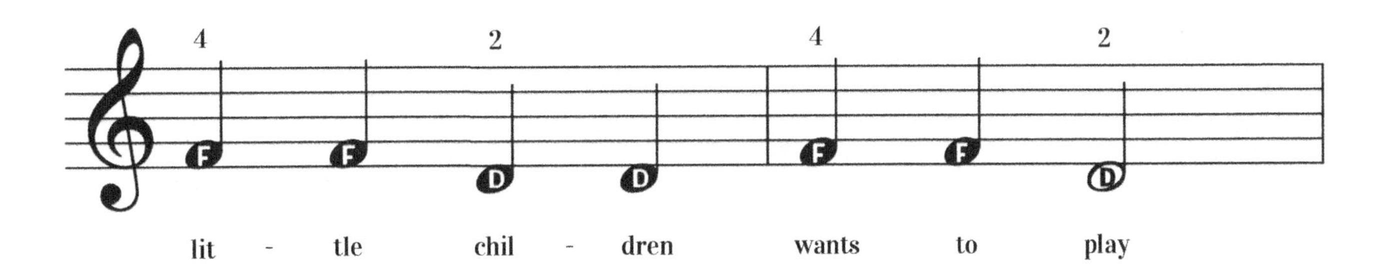

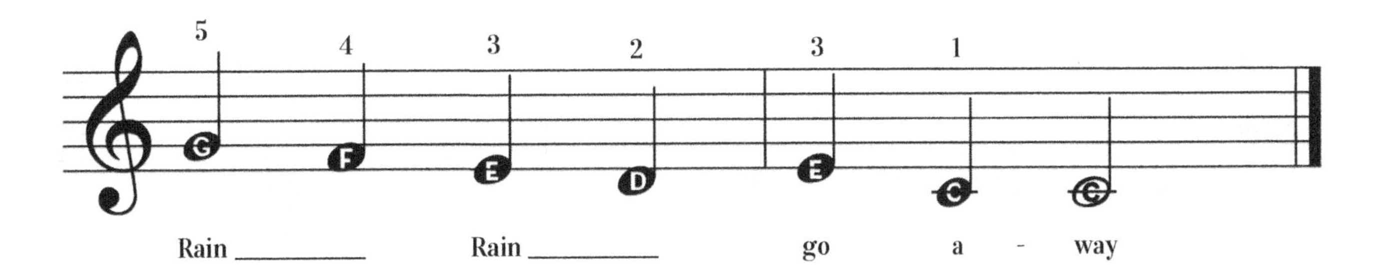

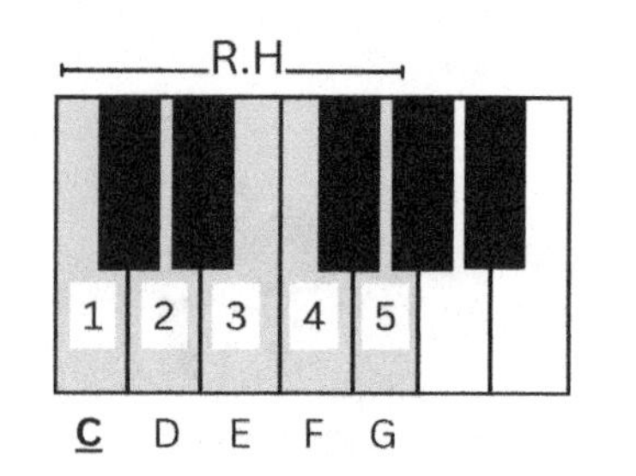

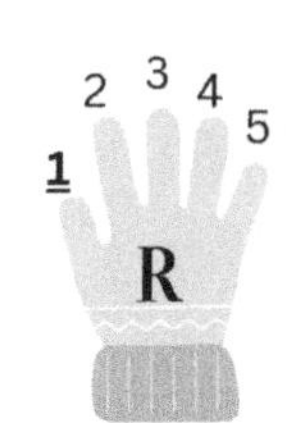

Ode to Joy

Ludwig van Beethoven

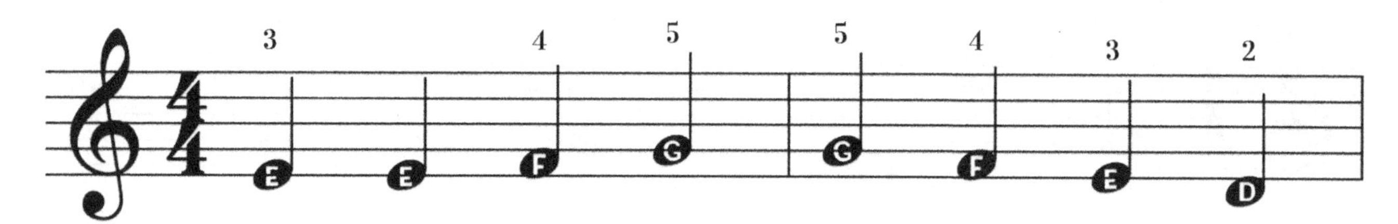

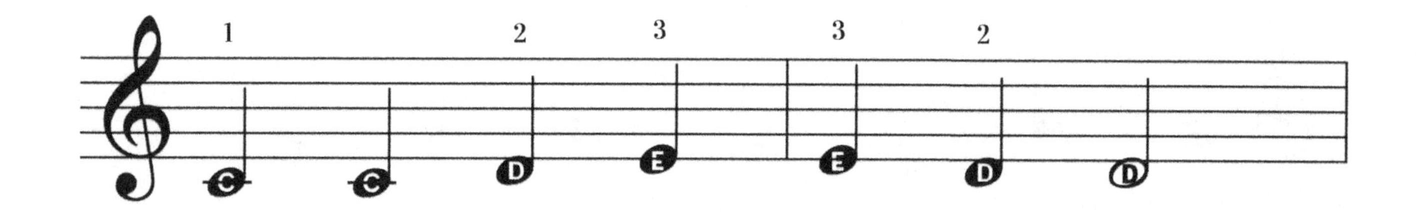

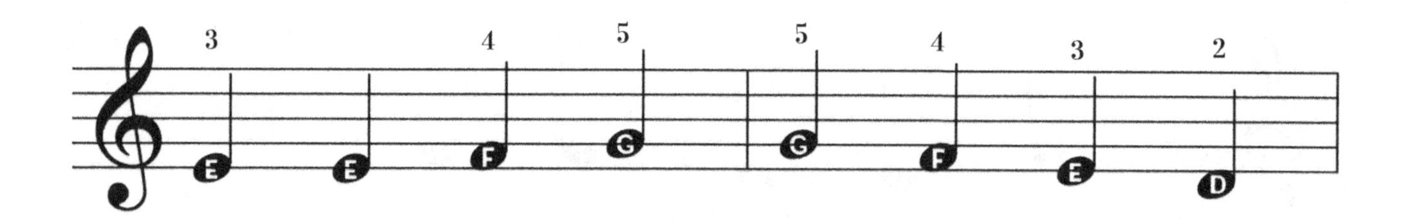

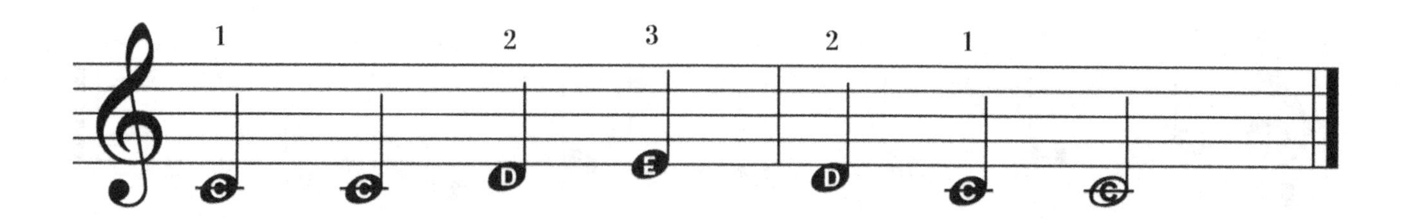

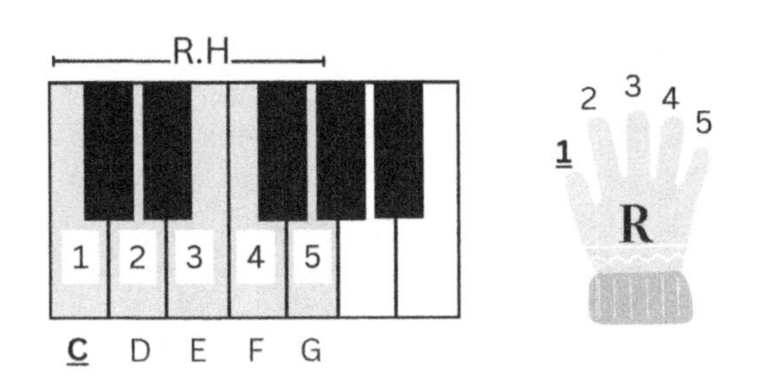

When The Saints Go Marching In

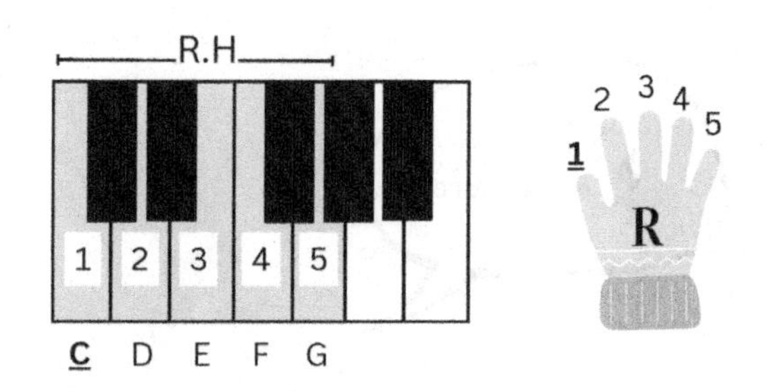

Jingle Bell

James Lord Pierpont

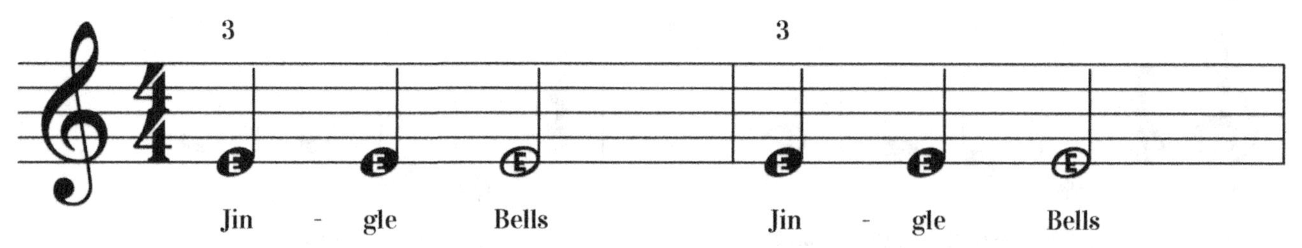

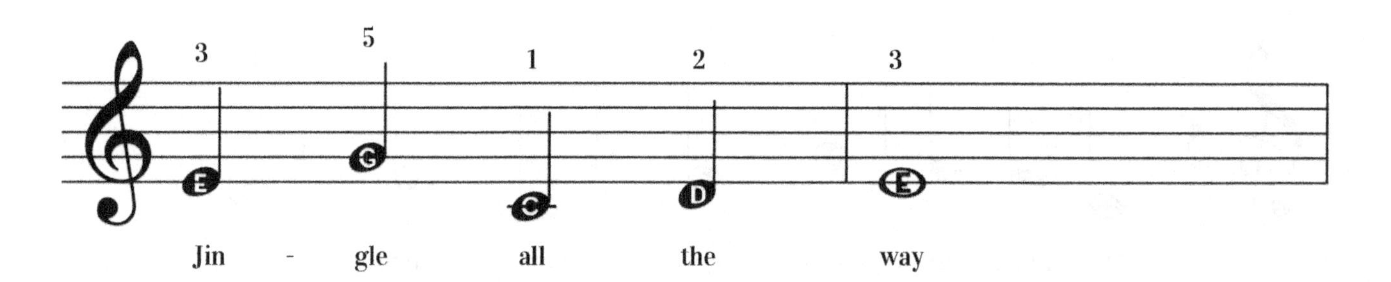

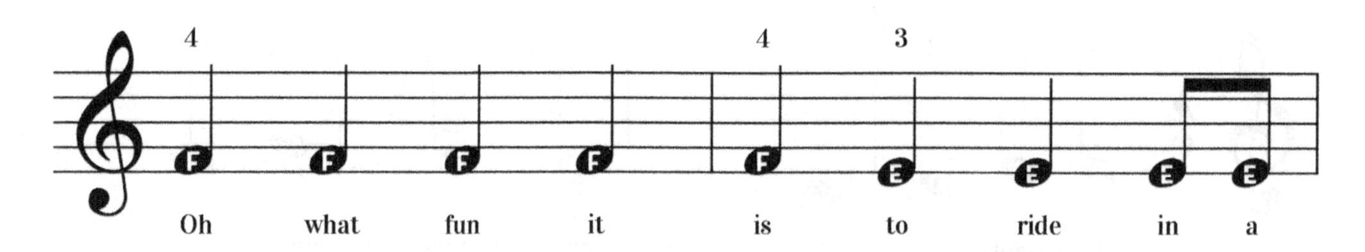

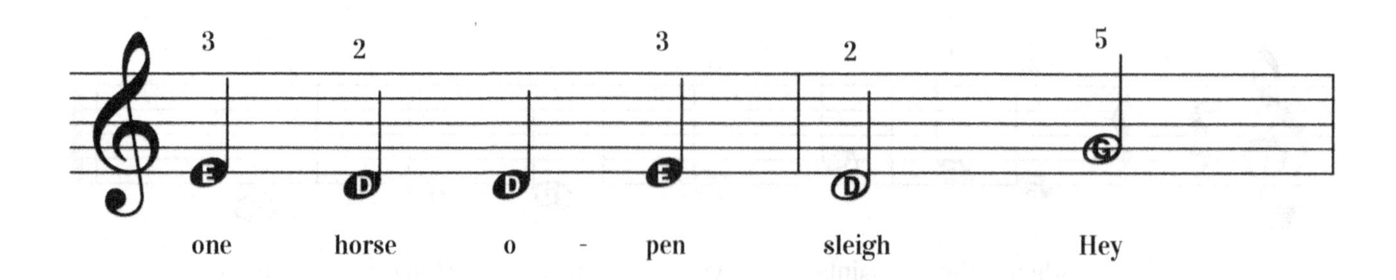

3
3
E E E E E E
Jin - gle Bells Jin - gle Bells
3 5 1 2 3
E G C D E
Jin - gle all the way
4 4 3
F F F F F E E E E
Oh what fun it is to ride in a
5 4 2 1
G G F D C
one horse o - pen sleigh
Do you know that "Jingle Bells" was actually a Thanksgiving tune. It was first sung at a Thanksgiving service in 1857.
Thanksgiving tuna? Now that's a holiday I can get behind!

Chapter 2

All songs in this chapter are written in the following hand position, so let's get familiar with it!

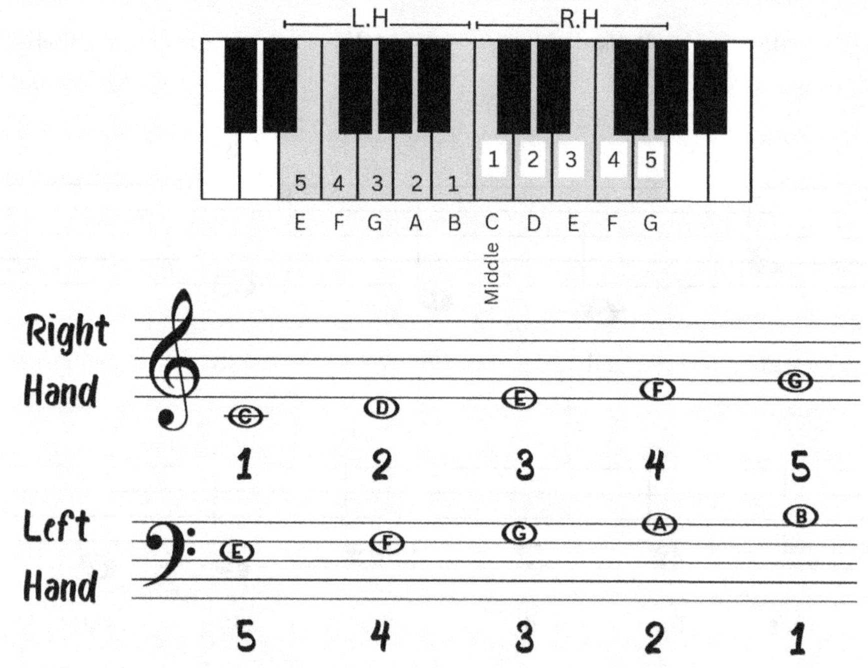

Name the keys! The first one is done for you already.

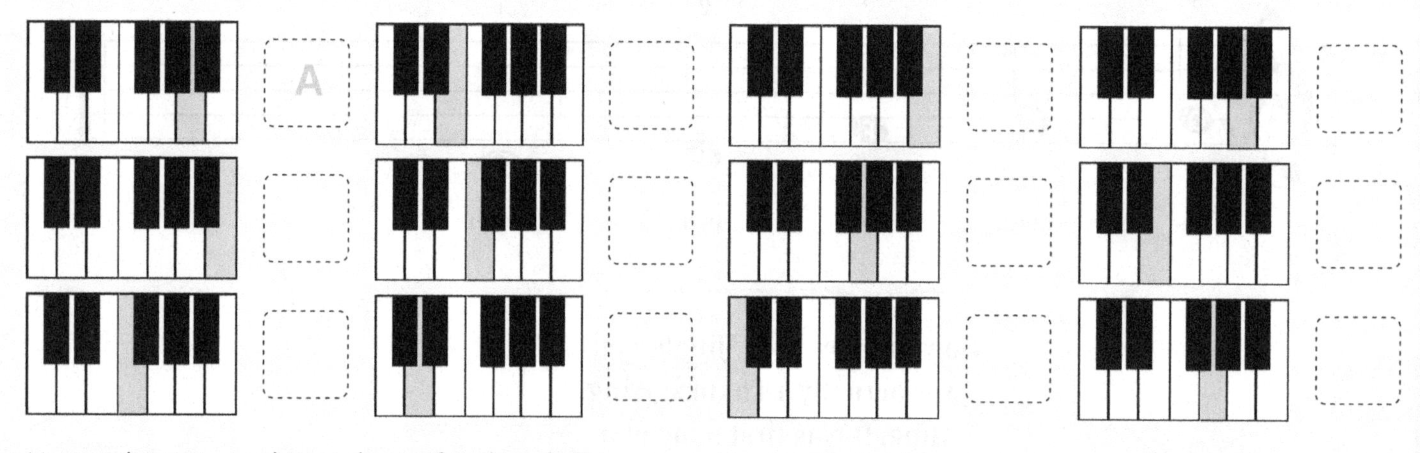

Name these notes! Watch out for the clef!

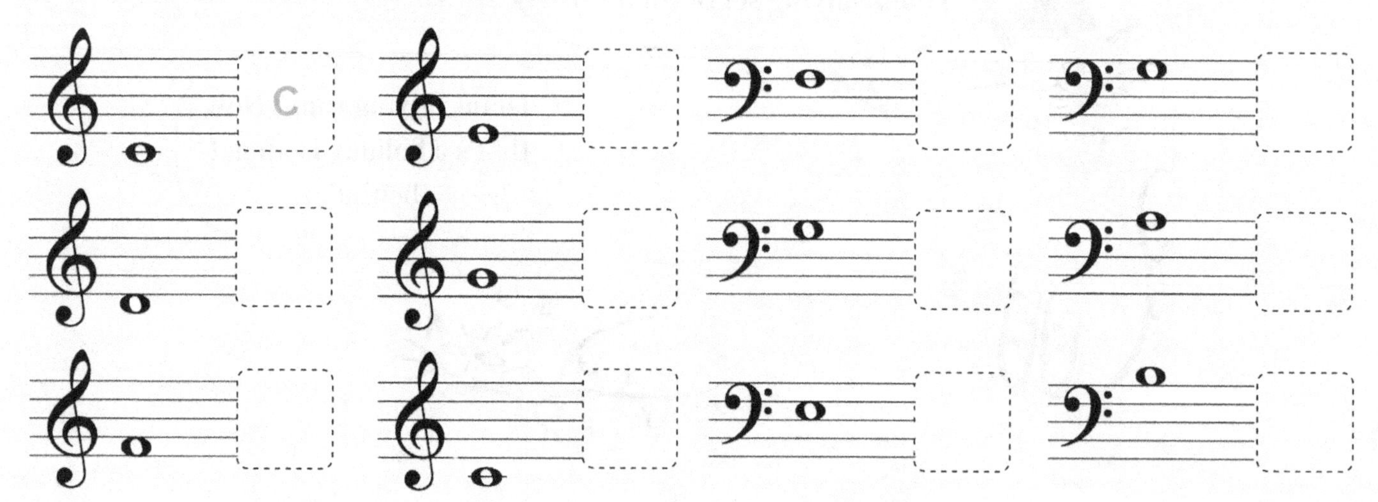

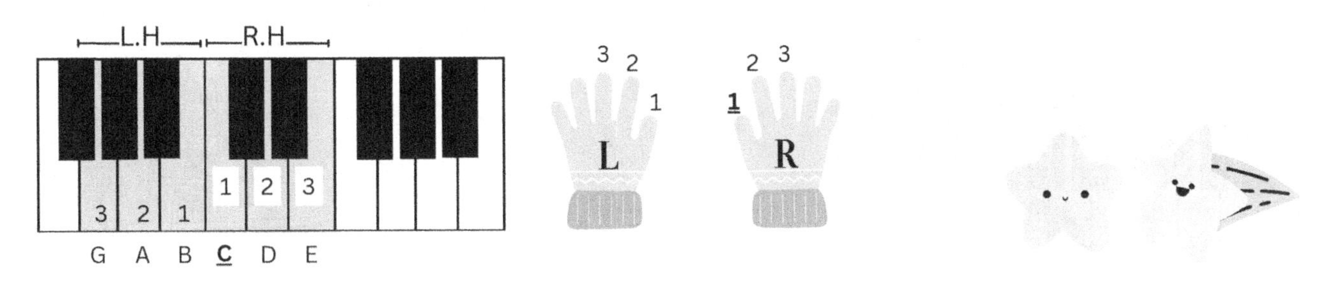

Right hand thumb on middle C
Left hand thumb on B

Twinkle Twinkle Little Star

Traditional

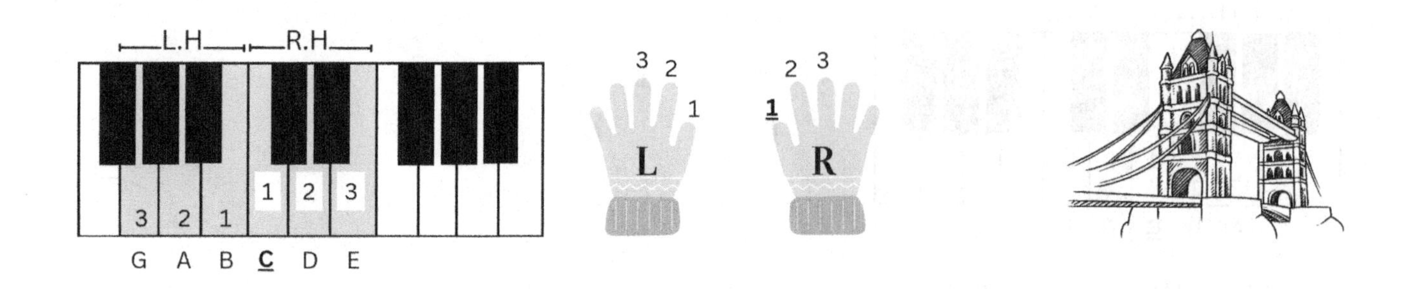

London Bridge

Traditional

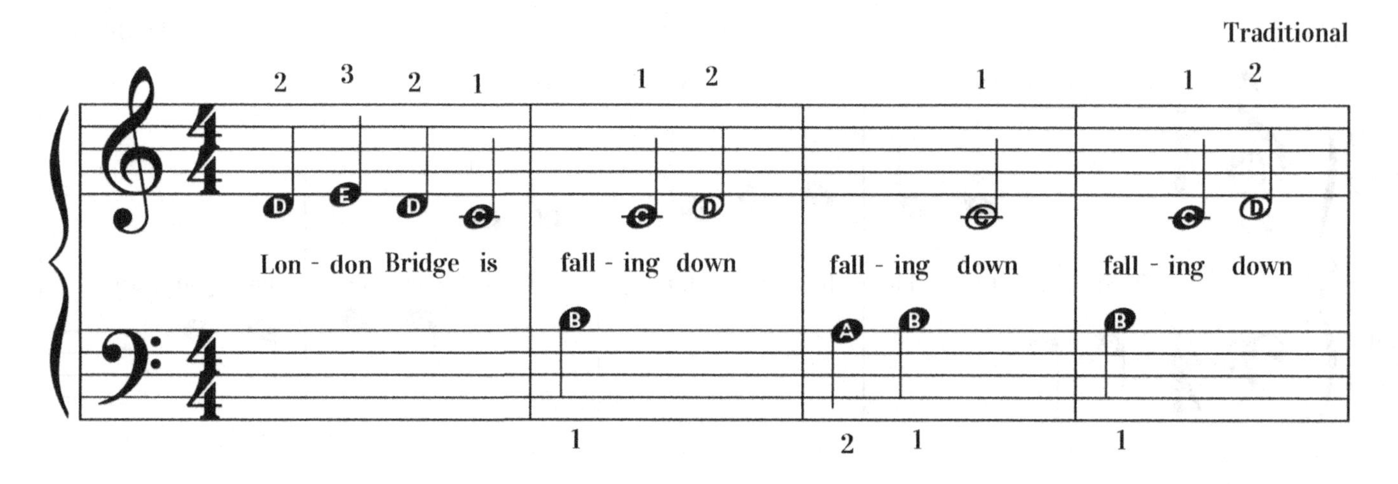

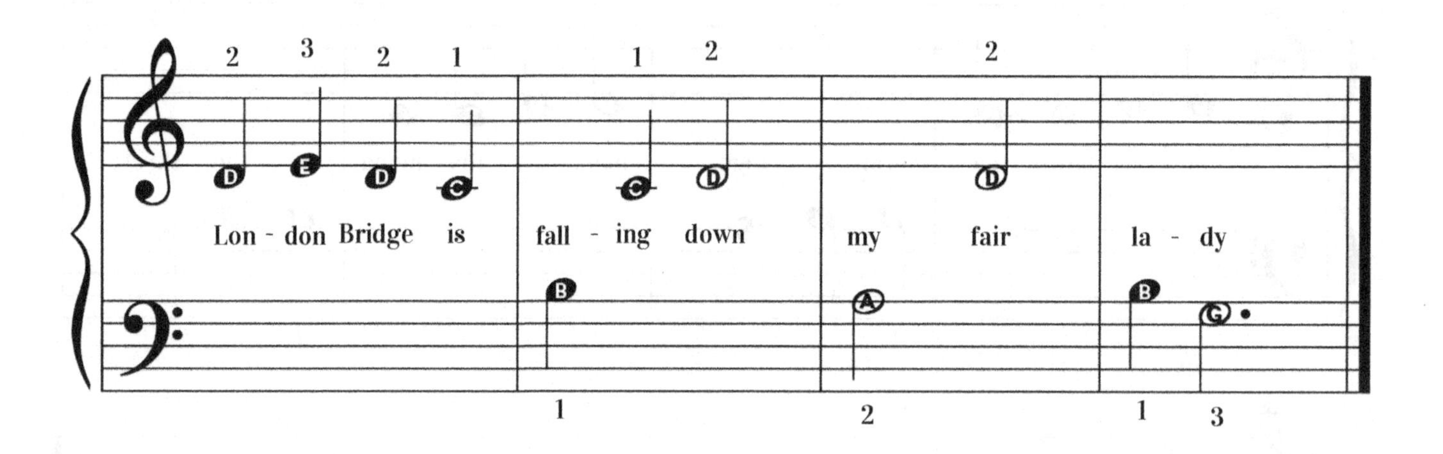

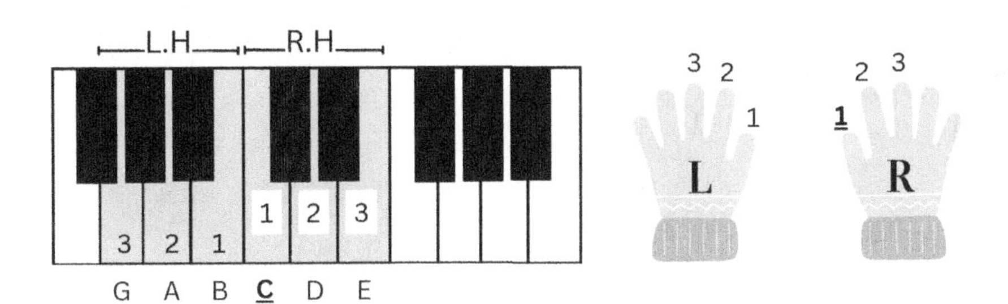

Baa Baa Black Sheep

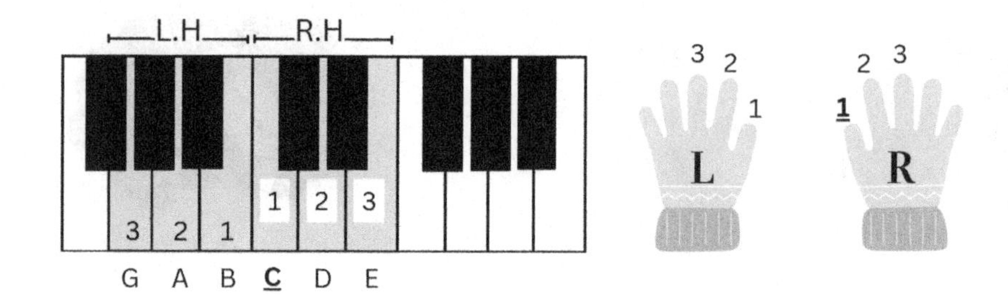

Oh Susanna

Stephen Foster

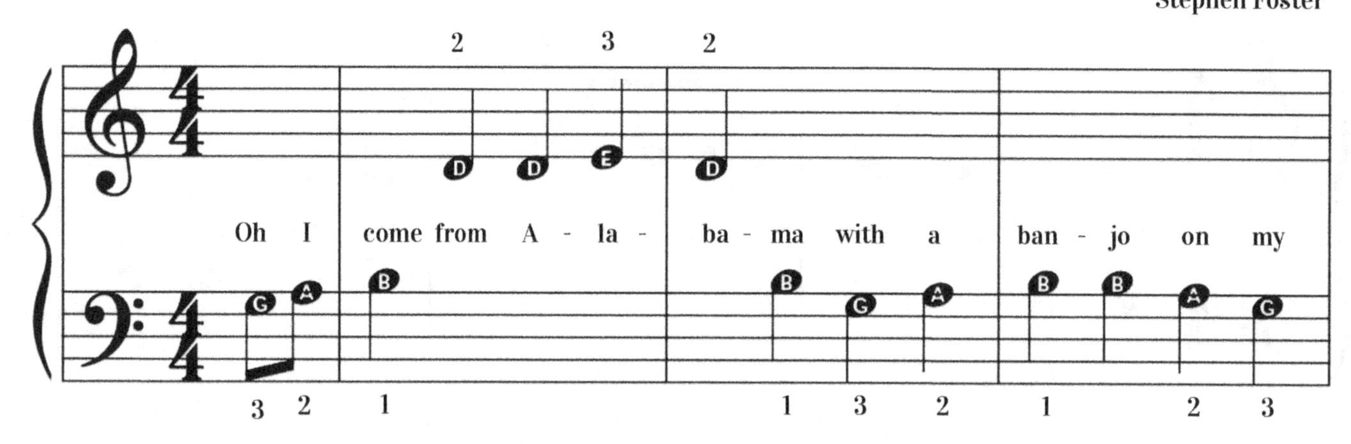

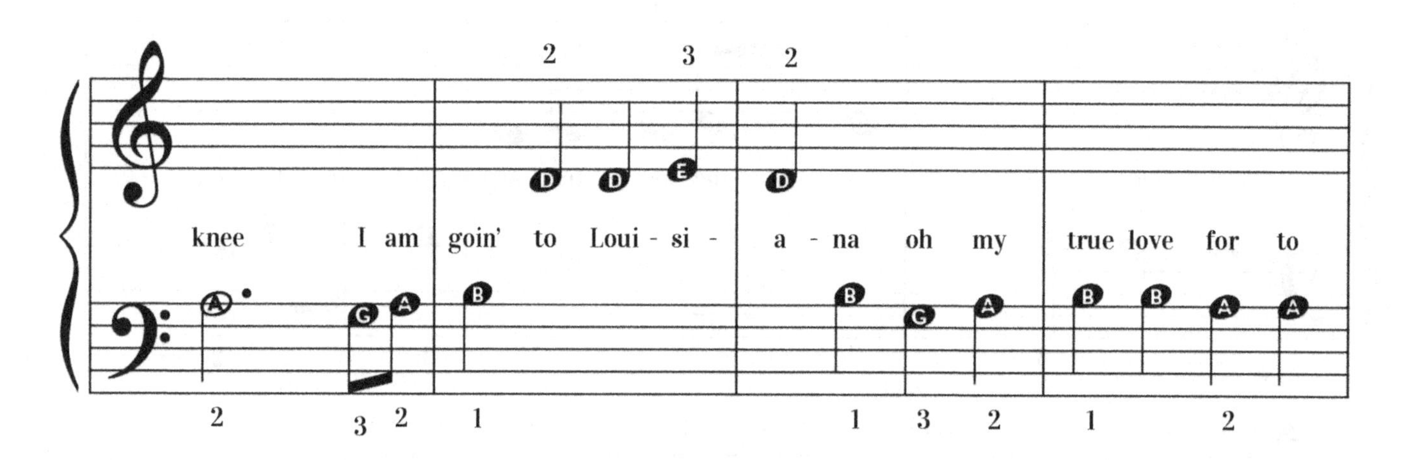

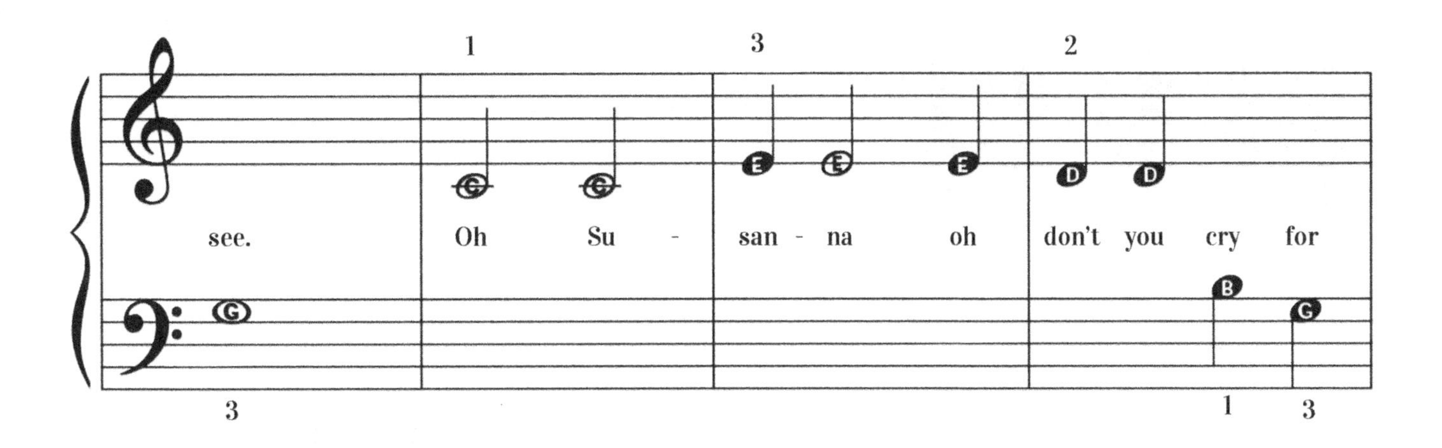
1 3 2
see. Oh Su - san - na oh don't you cry for
3 1 3

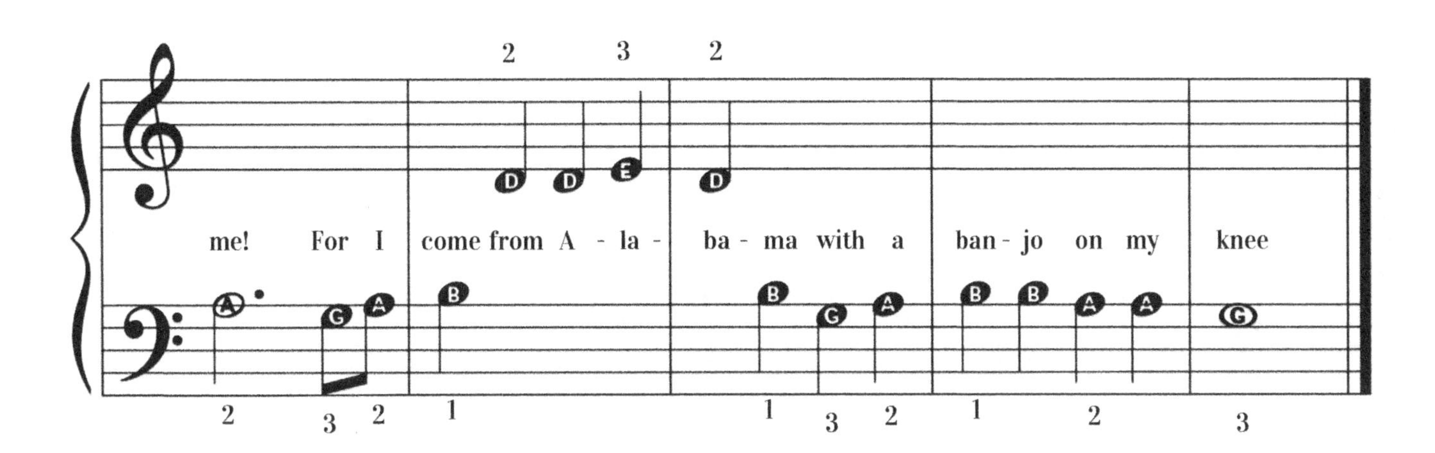
2 3 2
me! For I come from A - la - ba - ma with a ban - jo on my knee
2 3 2 1 1 3 2 1 2 3

Do you know that the piano's full name is actually "pianoforte"? It means "soft-loud" in Italian because it can play notes softly (piano) and loudly (forte).
Soft-loud? So it's like when I softly sneak up on you and then loudly knock over a vase after?

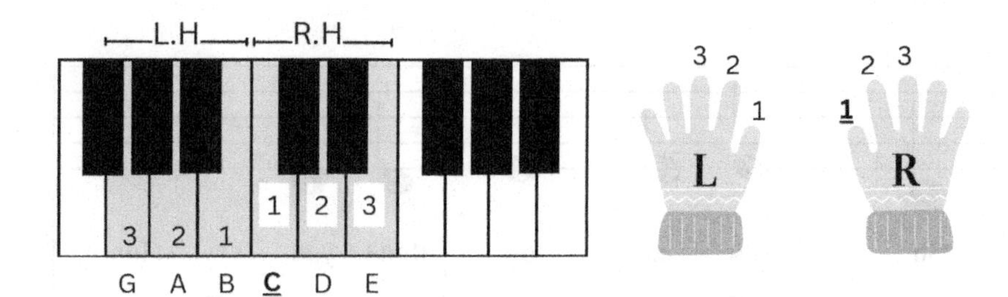

Old Mcdonald Had a Farm

Traditional

1
1
1
moo moo there
here a moo there a moo
E - very-where a moo moo

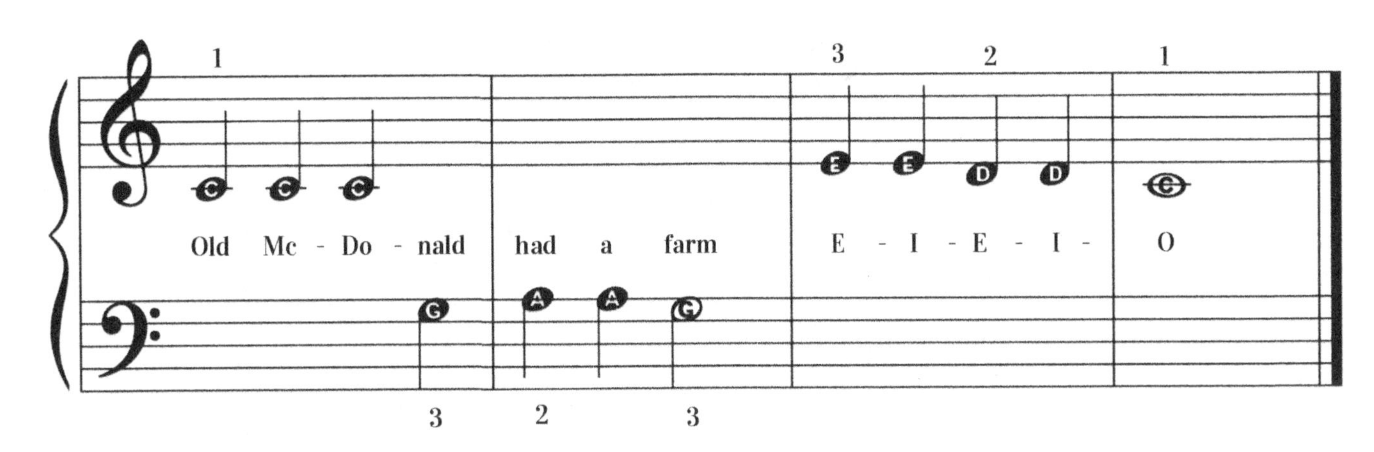
1
3
2
1
Old Mc - Do - nald
had a farm
E - I - E - I -
O
3
2
3

Albert Einstein said "Anyone who has never made a mistake has never tried anything new!"
Yeah, but I've purr-fected the art of looking adorable while doing it!

Unlock the 4 digit password by decoding the rhythm. For example ♩ = 1 𝅗𝅥 = 2 𝅗𝅥. = 3 𝅝 = 4

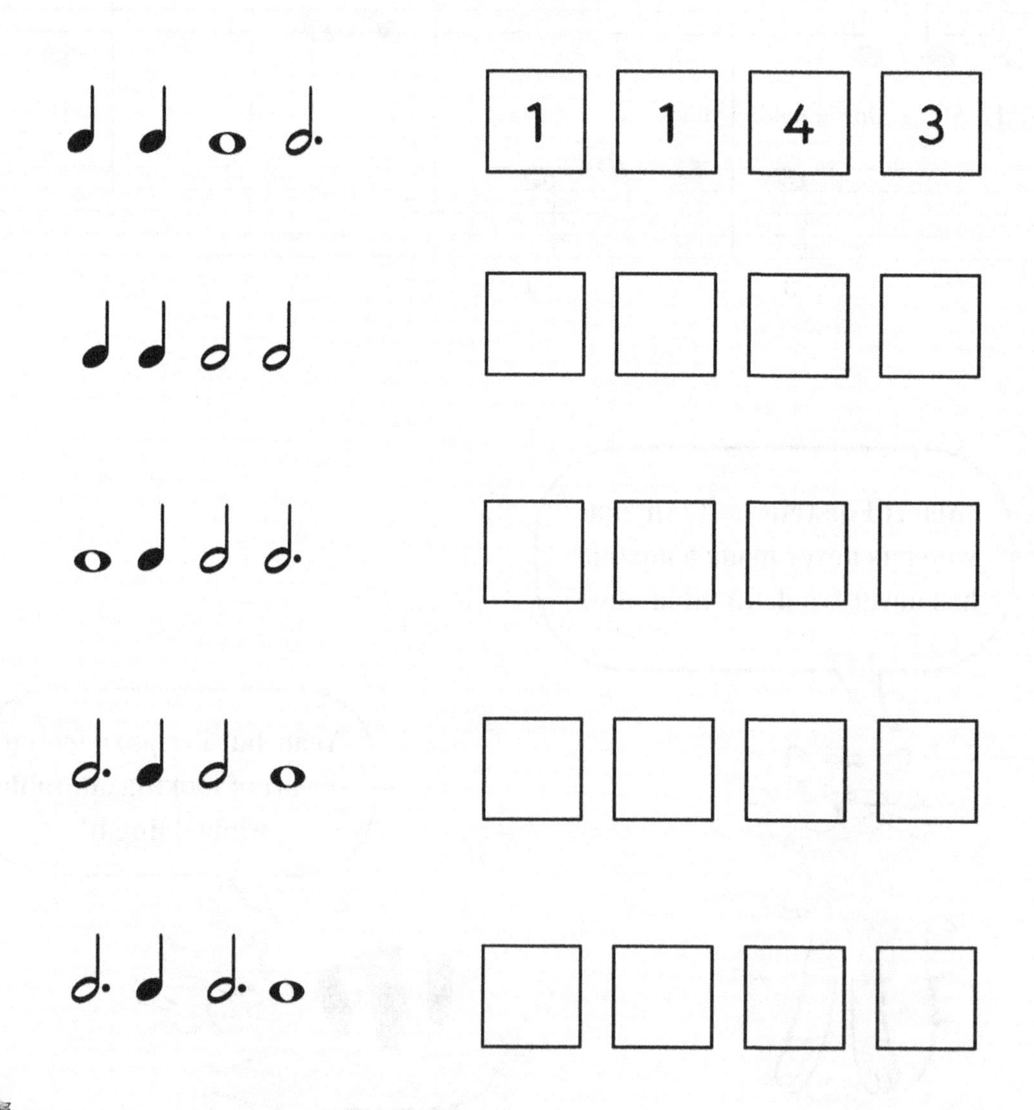

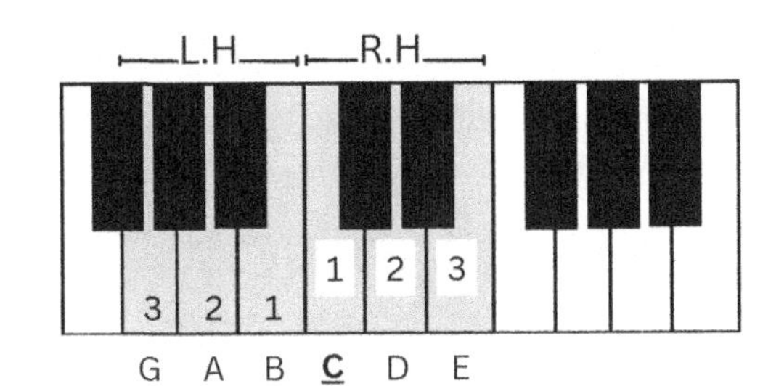

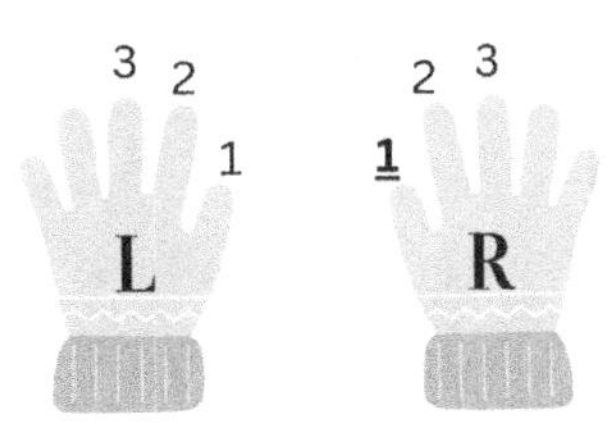

Muffin Man

Traditional

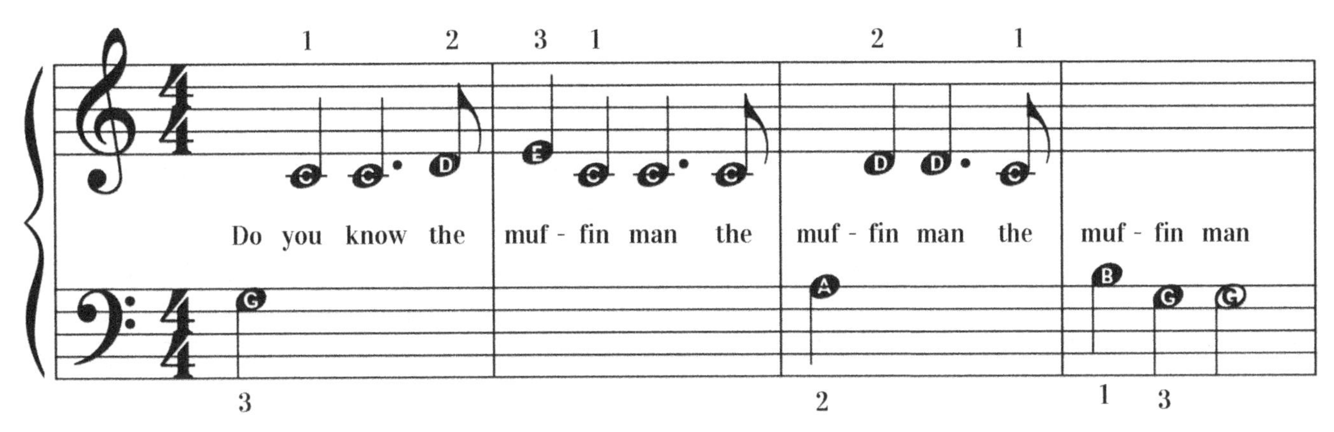

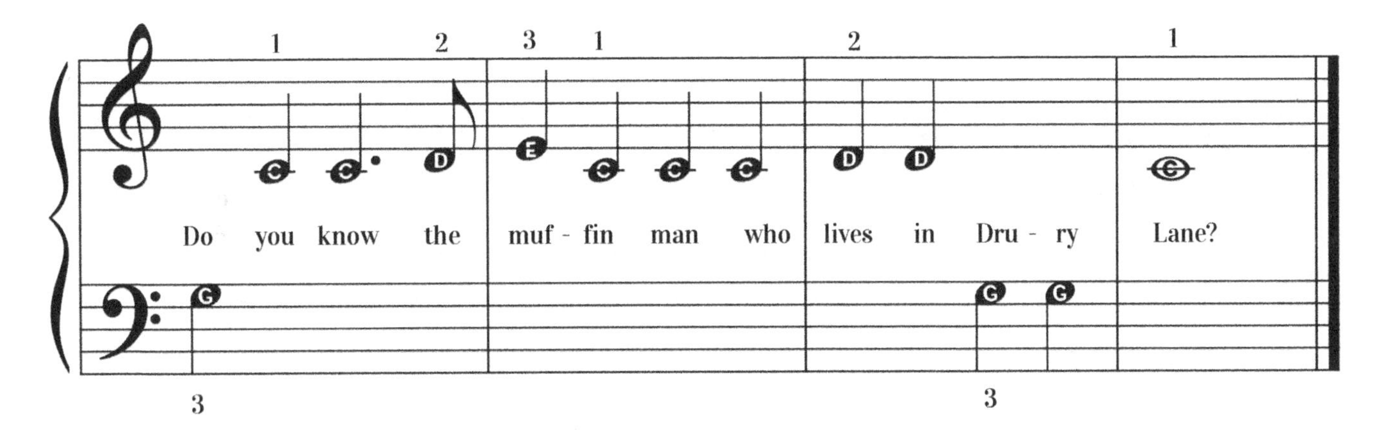

Yo! Clap and count this rhythm before you play the song. It will help you play those dotted quarter notes!

1 n 2 n 3 n 4 n | 1 n 2 n 3 n 4 n

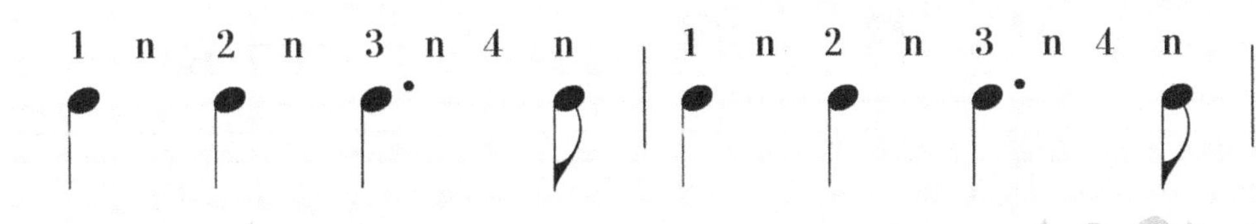

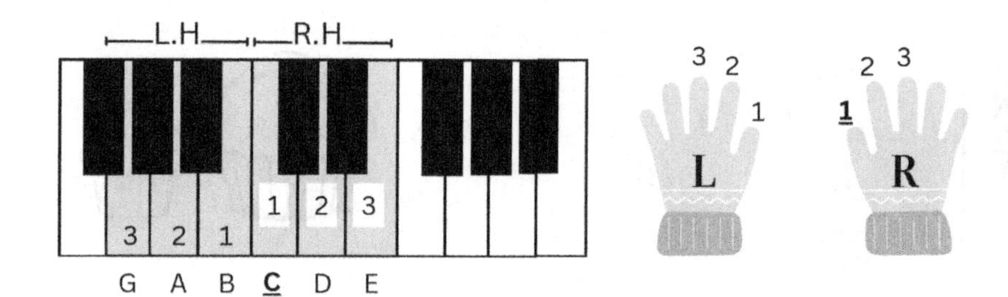

Ring Around The Rosie

Traditional

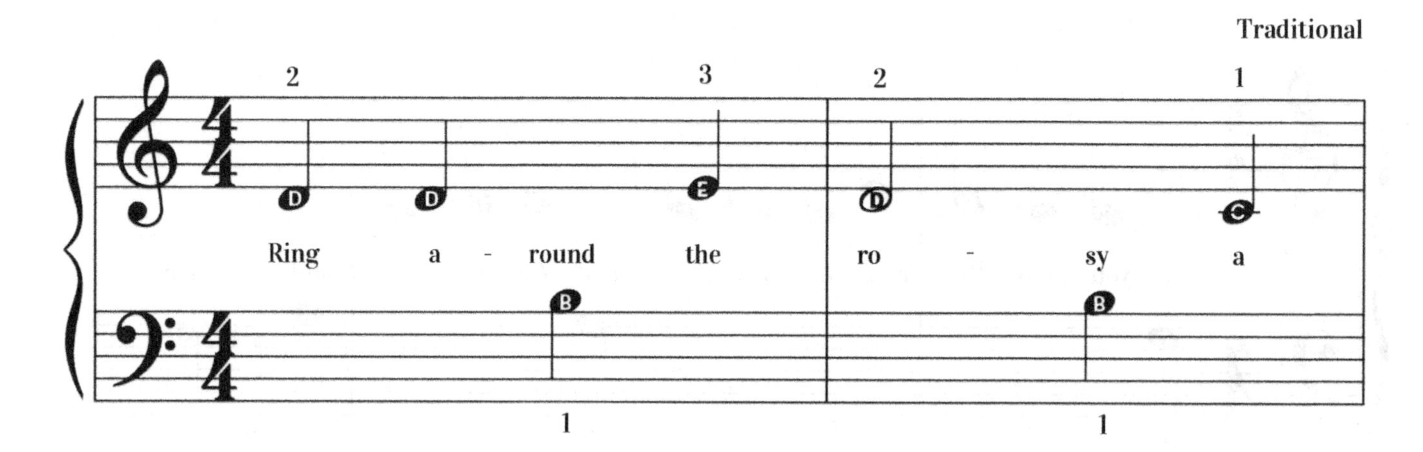

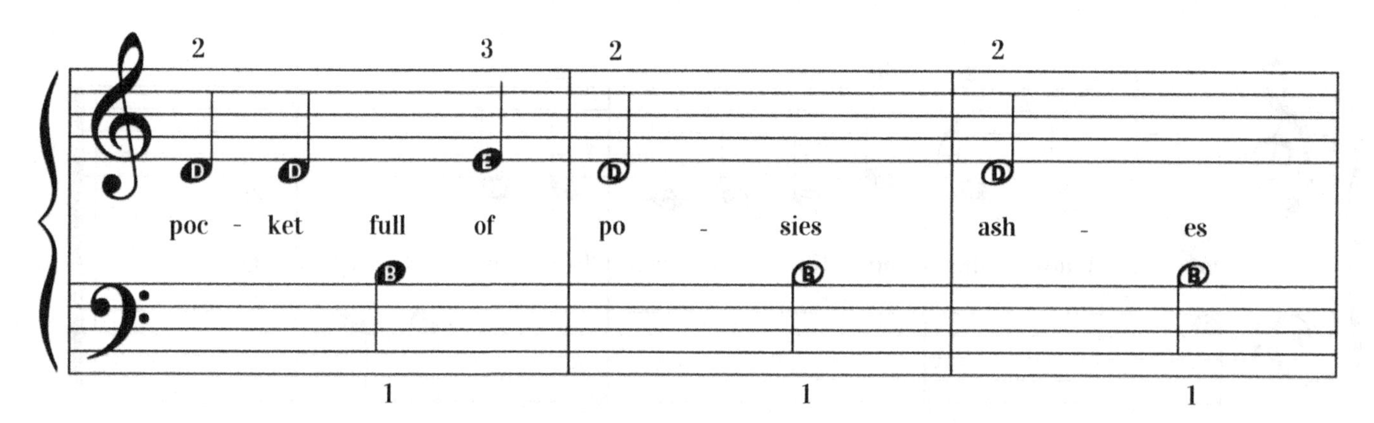

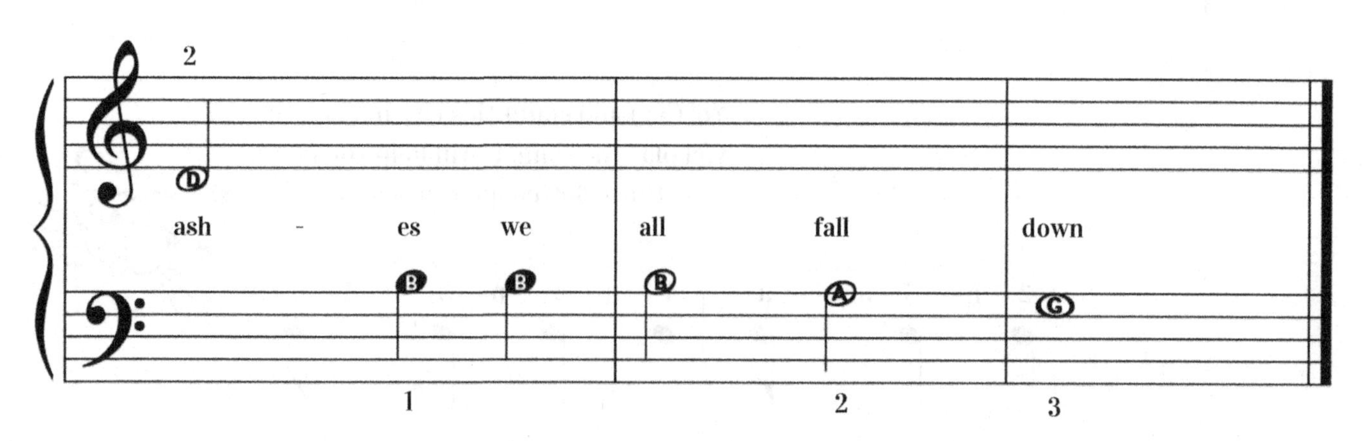

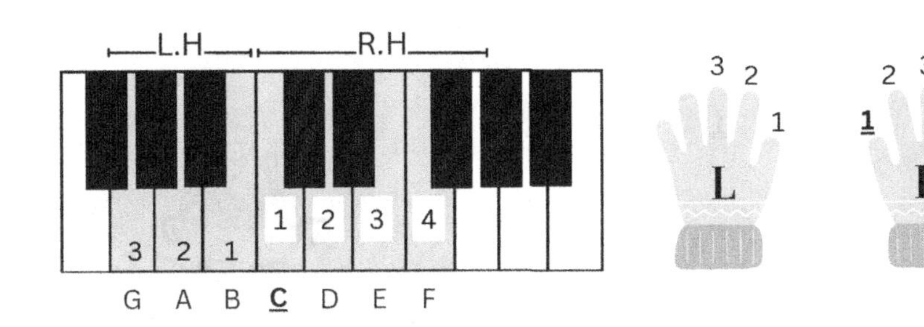

B-I-N-G-O

Traditional

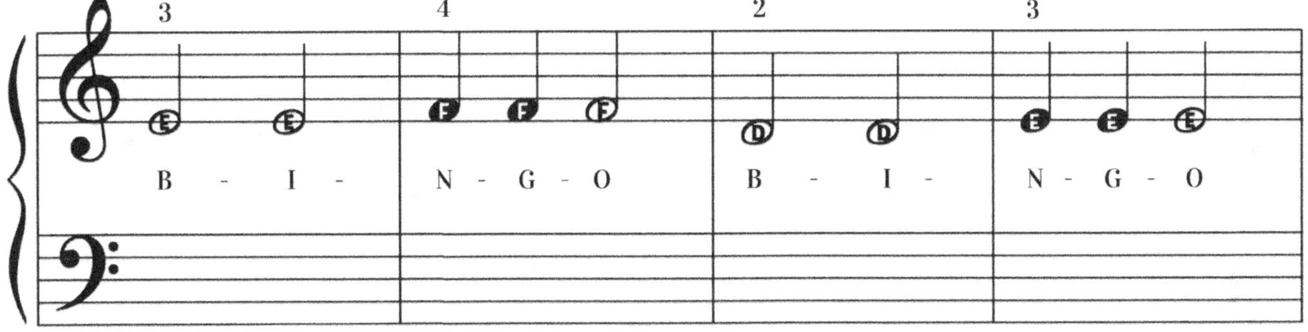

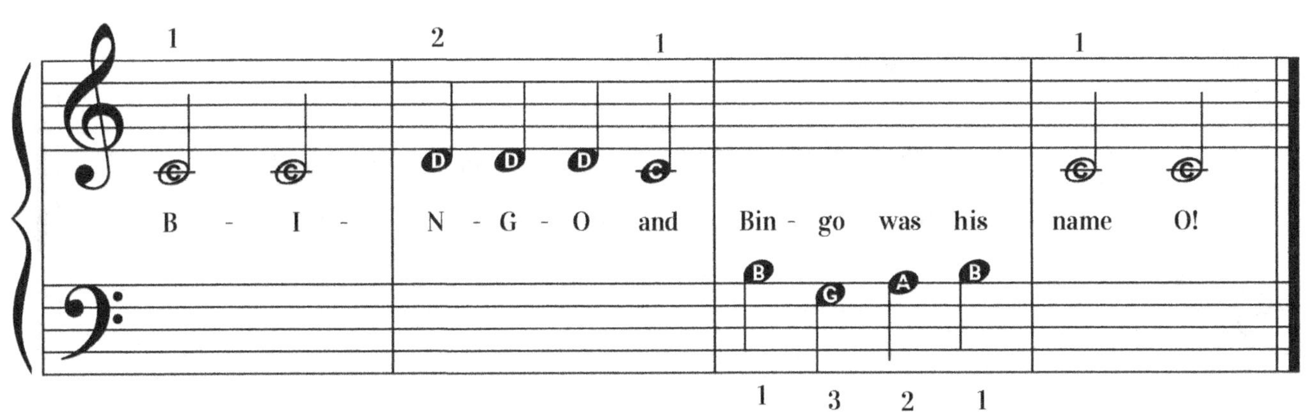

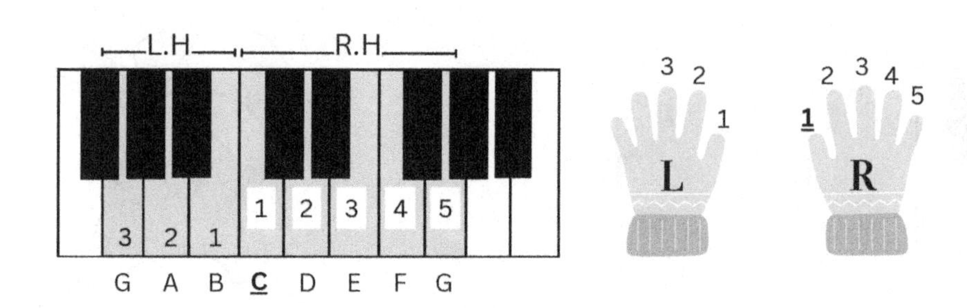

Happy Birthday

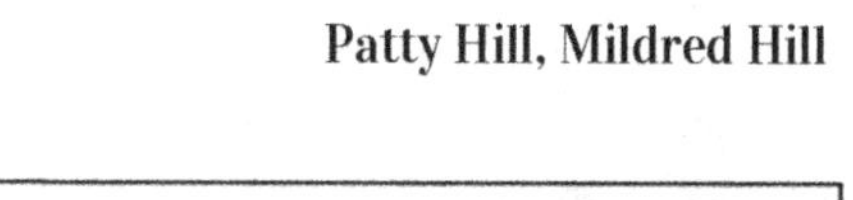

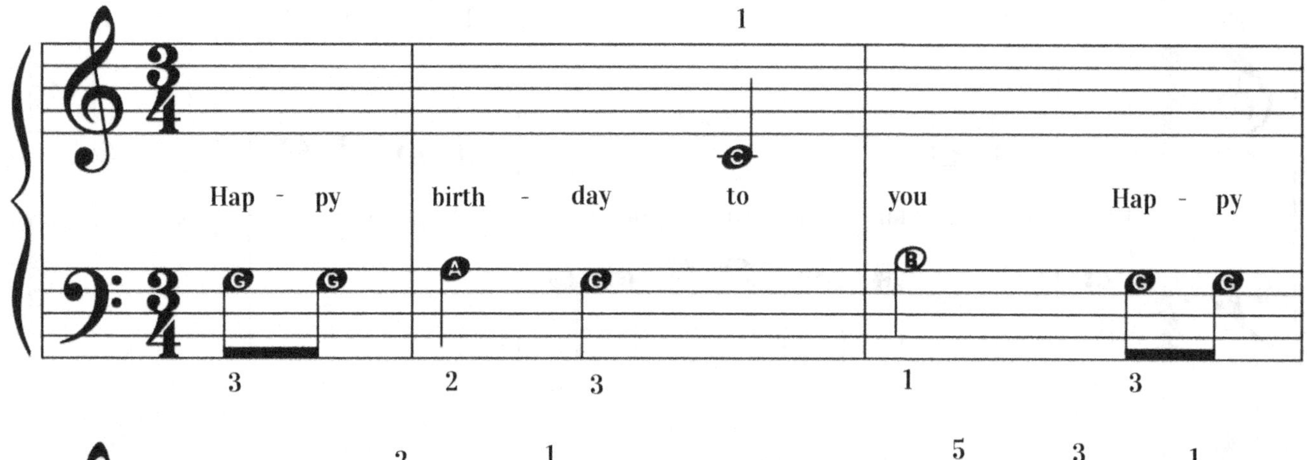

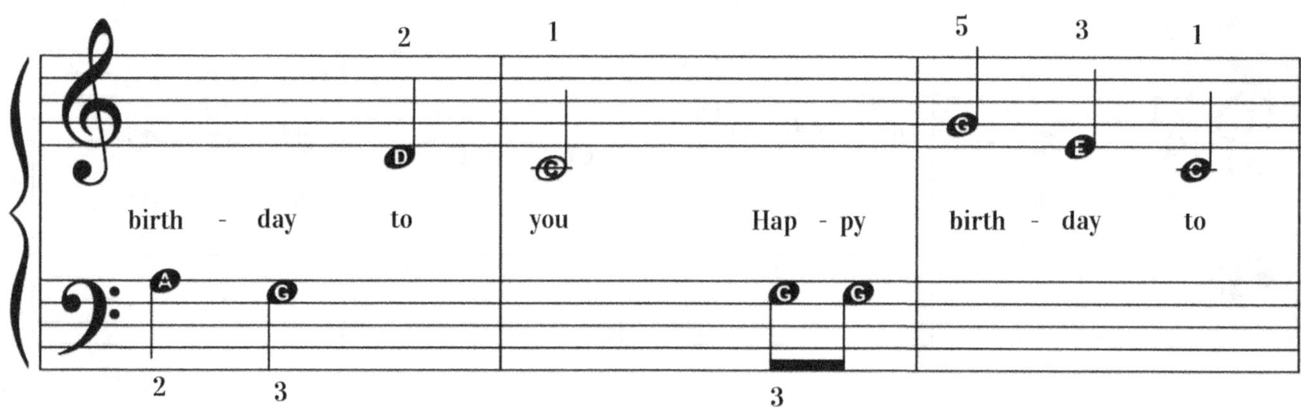

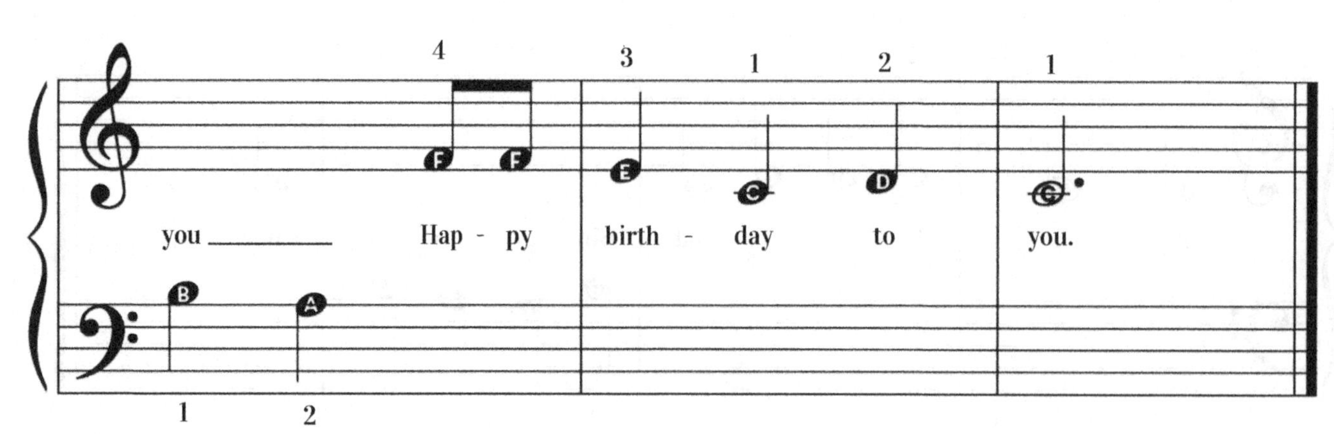

Follow the path with the correct notes, circle them and use your answers to guide you to the end of the maze where you can make an escape. The first one is done for you.

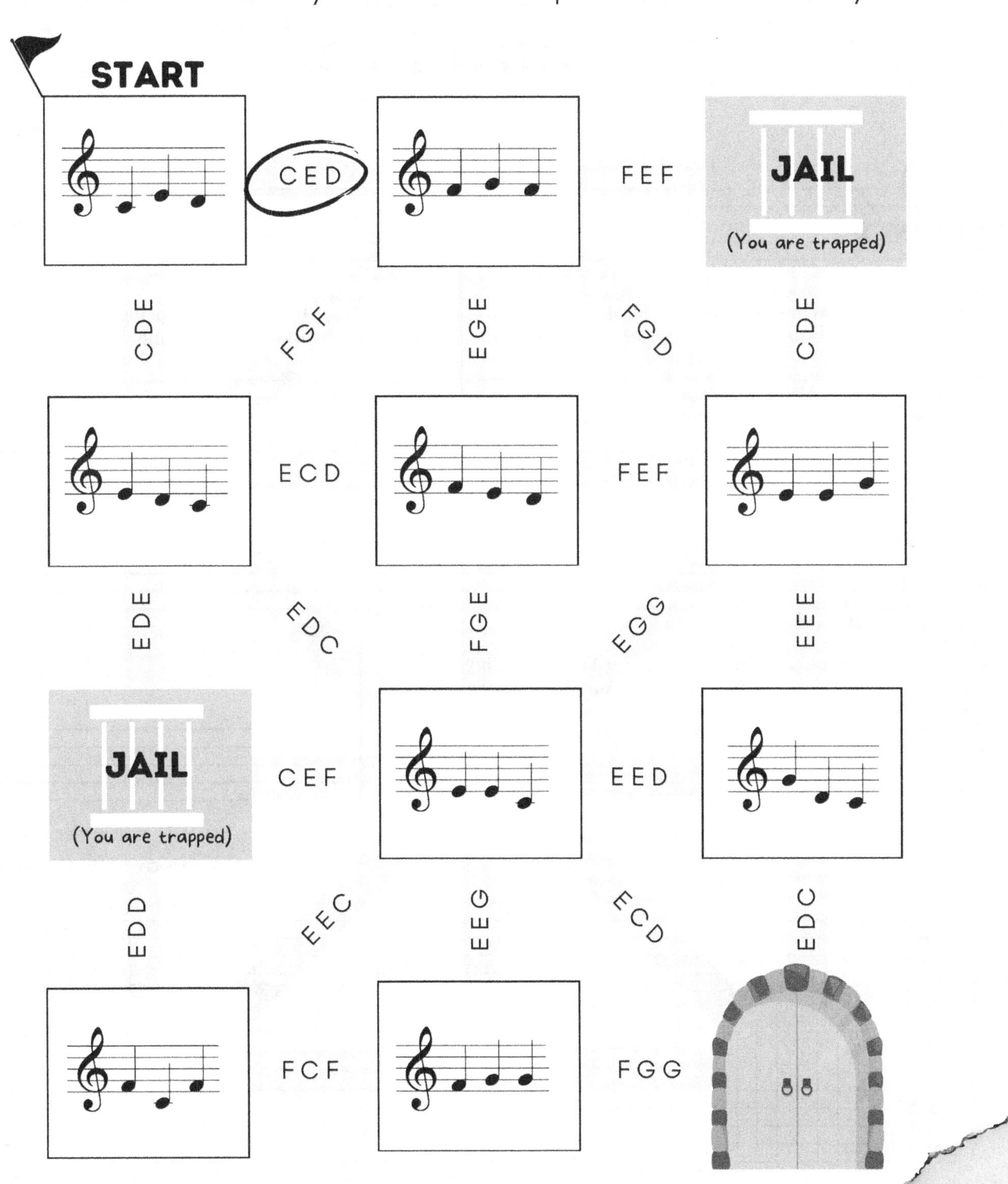

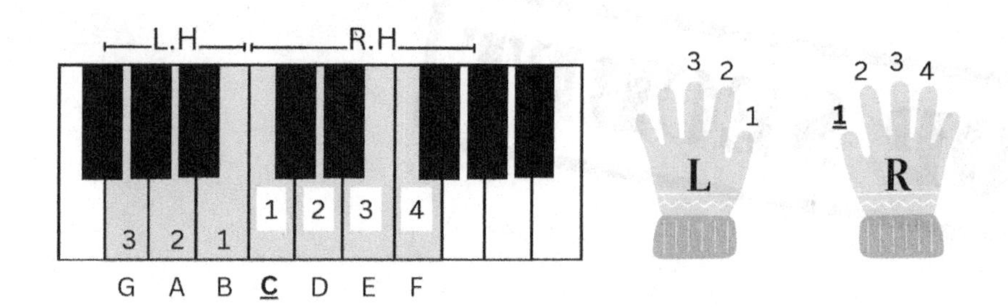

Aura Lea

George R. Poulton

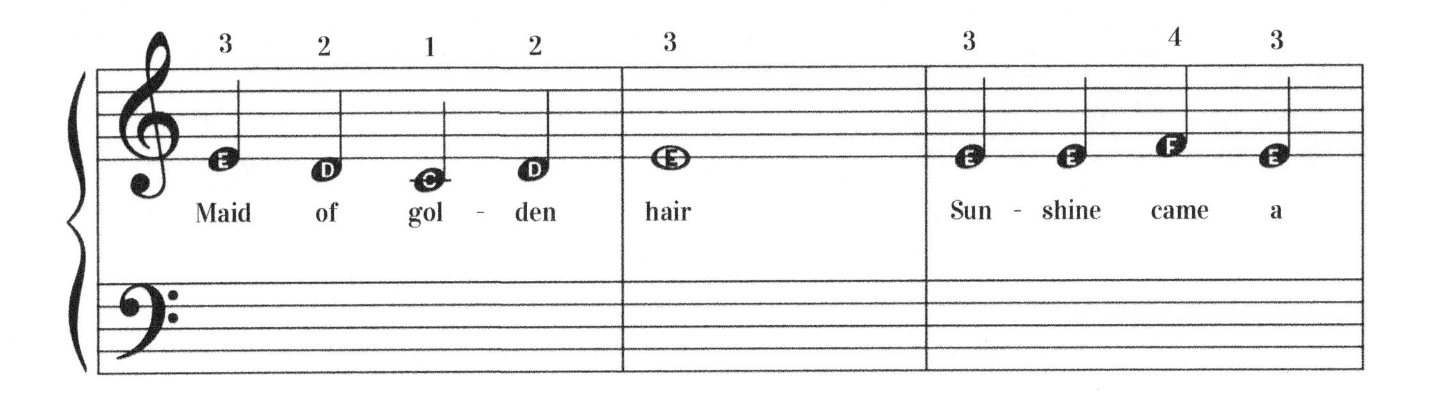
3 2 1 2 3 3 3 4 3
E D C D E E E F E
Maid of gol - den hair Sun - shine came a

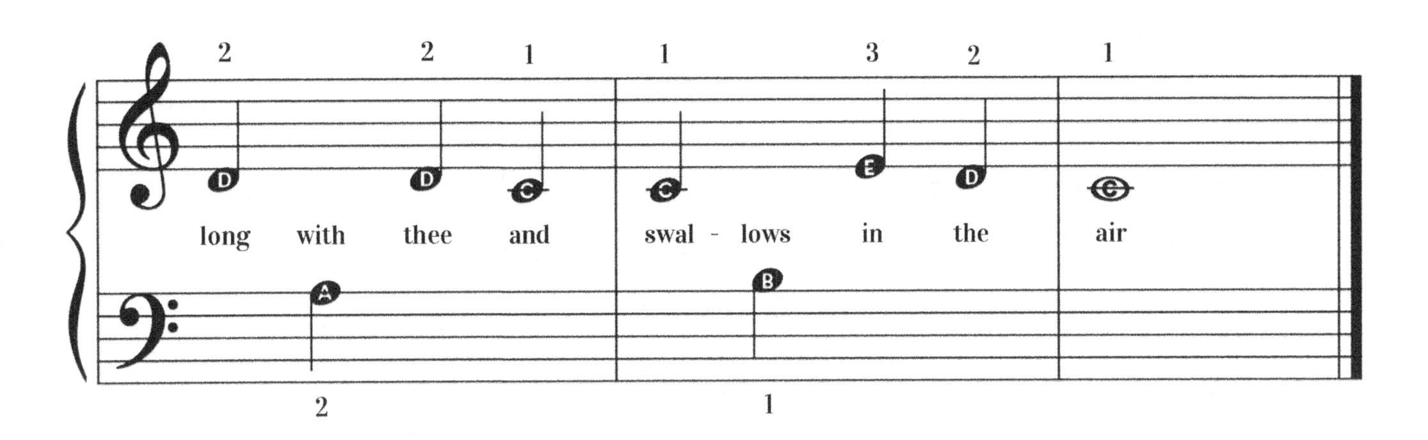
2 2 1 1 3 2 1
D D C C E D C
long with thee and swal - lows in the air
A B
2 1

Do you know Carlos Martinez hold the World Record for the longest piano playing? He played for 127 hours straight! That's over 5 days of non-stop playing!
127 hours? I can't even stay awake for 1 hour without a nap!

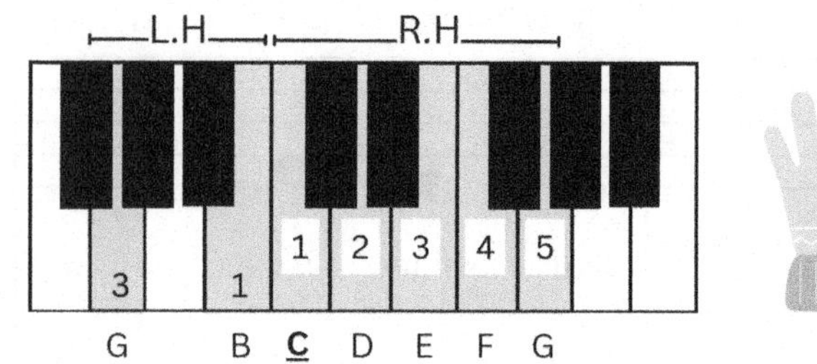

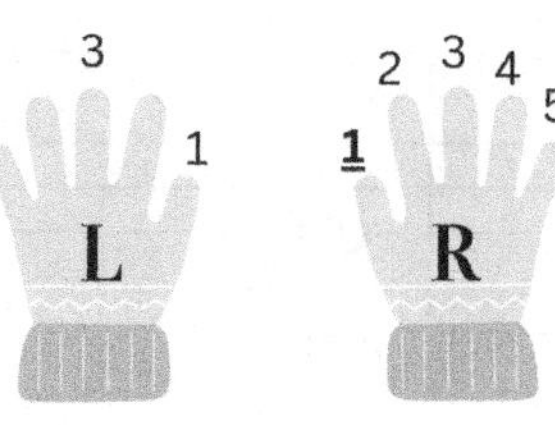

Clementine

Percy Montrose

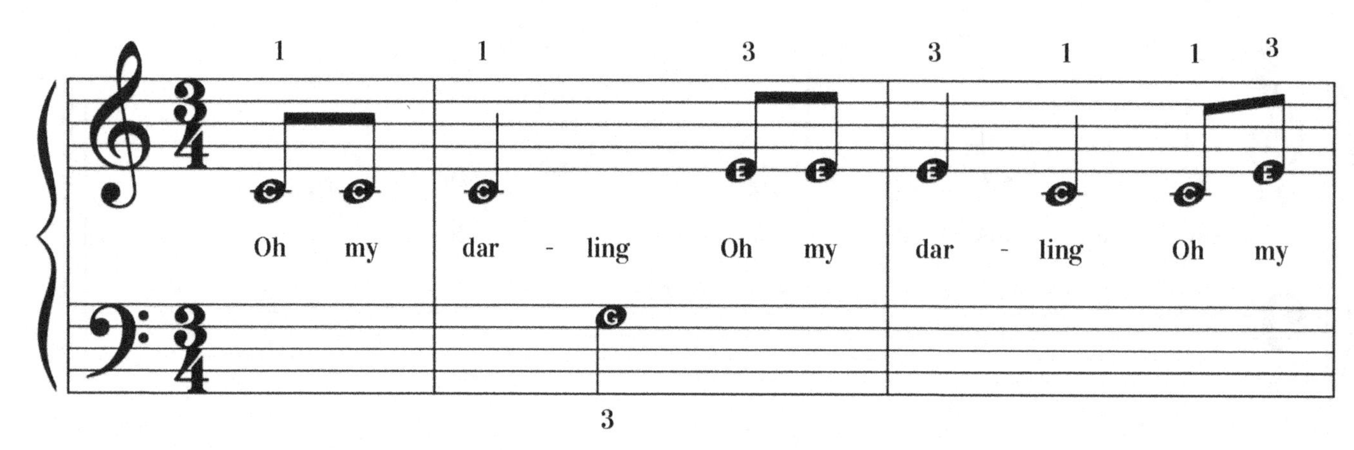

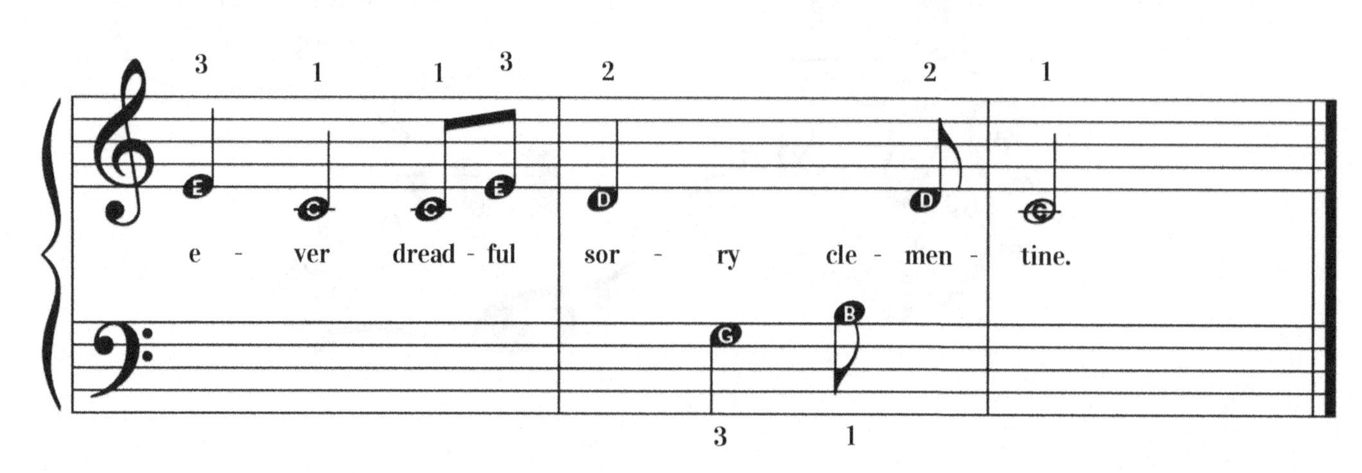

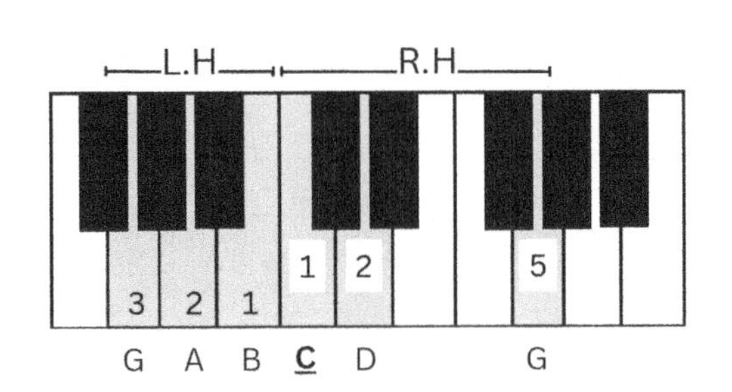

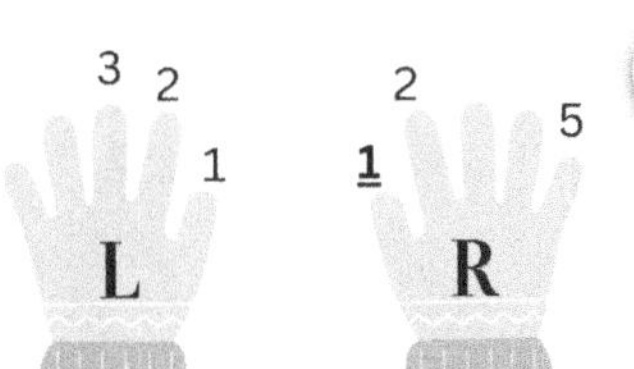

Row Row Row Your Boat

Traditional

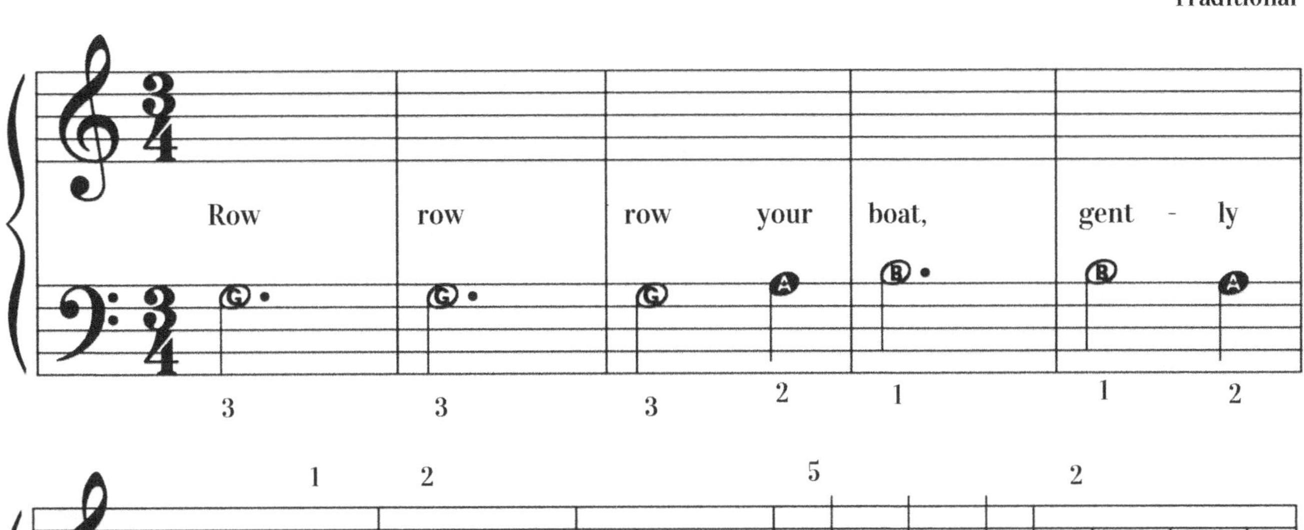

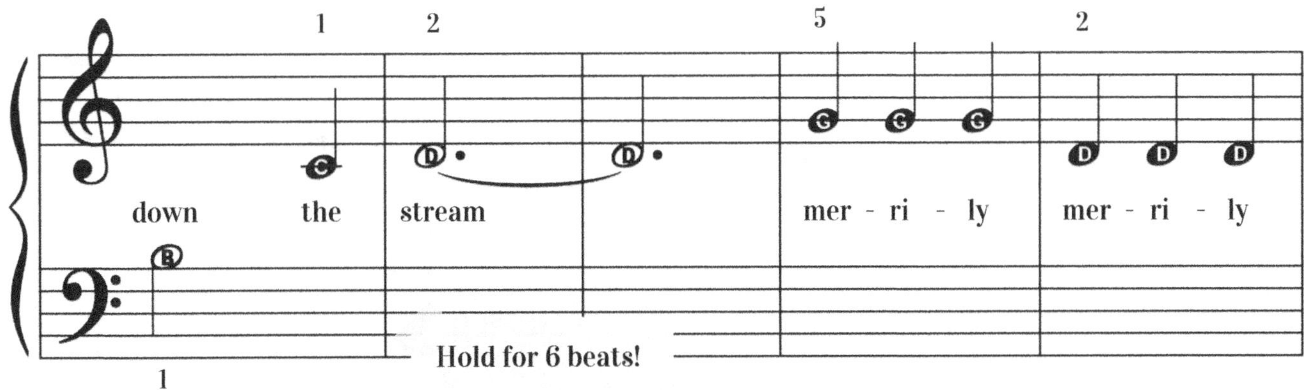

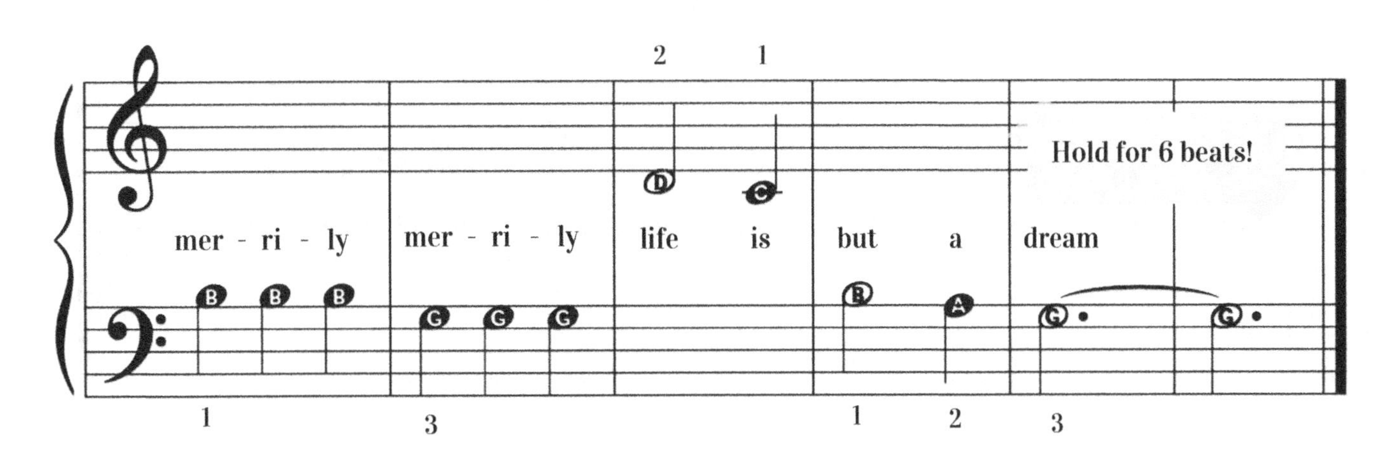

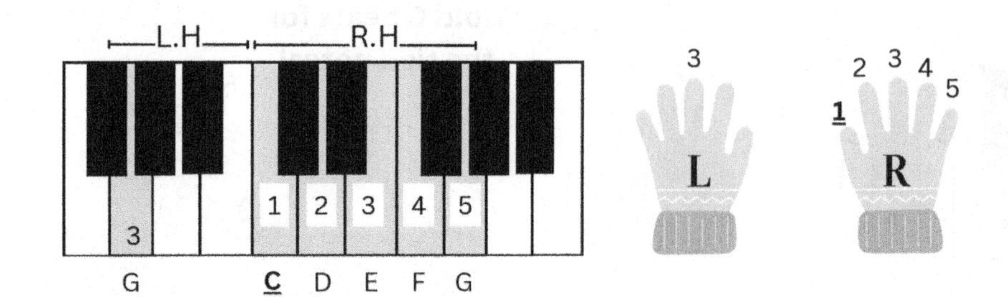

Five Little Monkeys

Traditional

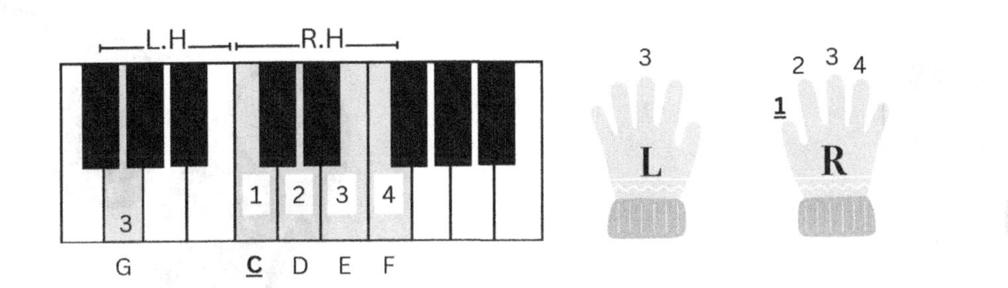

Hush Little Baby

Traditional

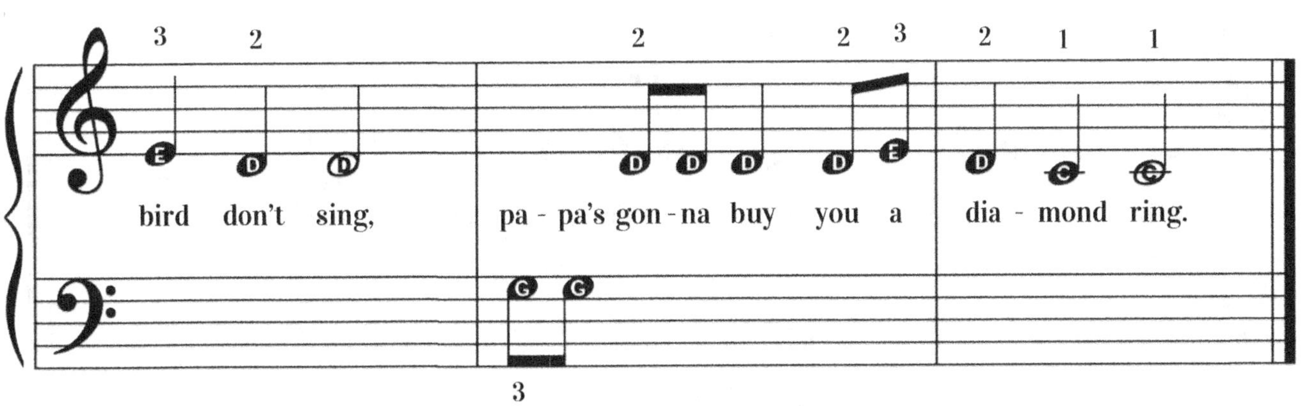

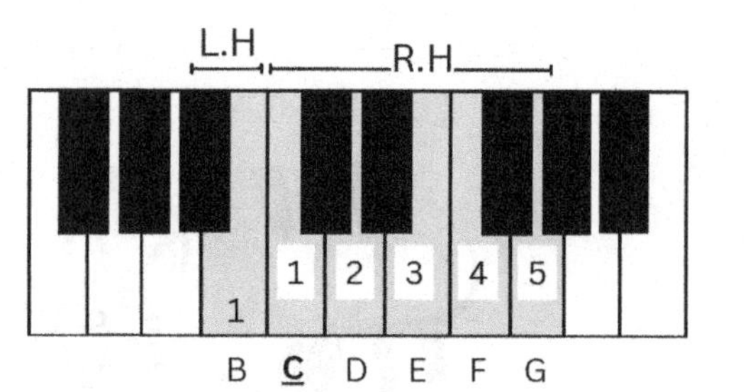

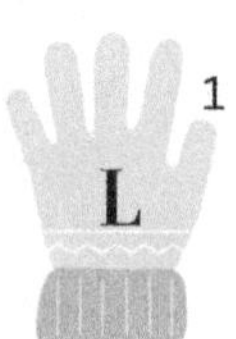

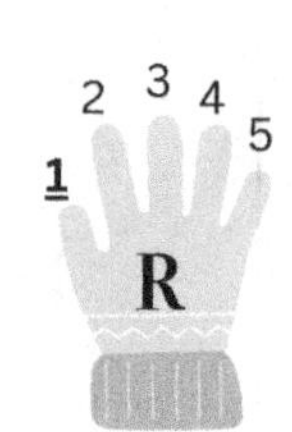

Skip To My Lou

Traditional

3 1 3 5

Lou Lou skip to my Lou,

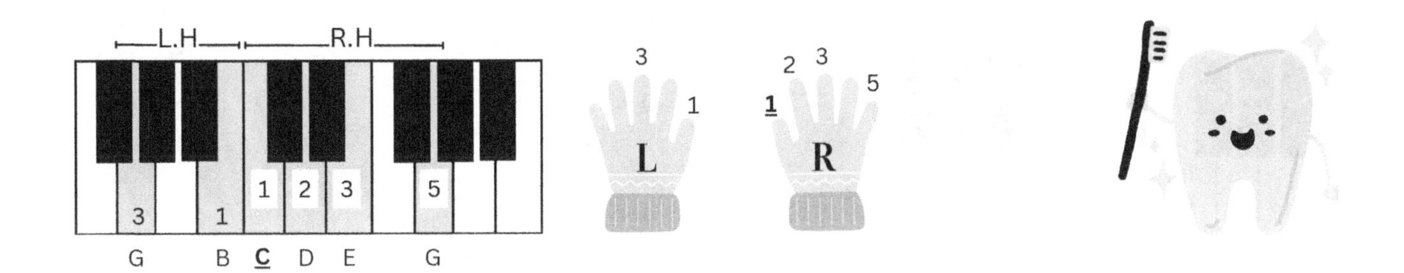

This is the way

Traditional

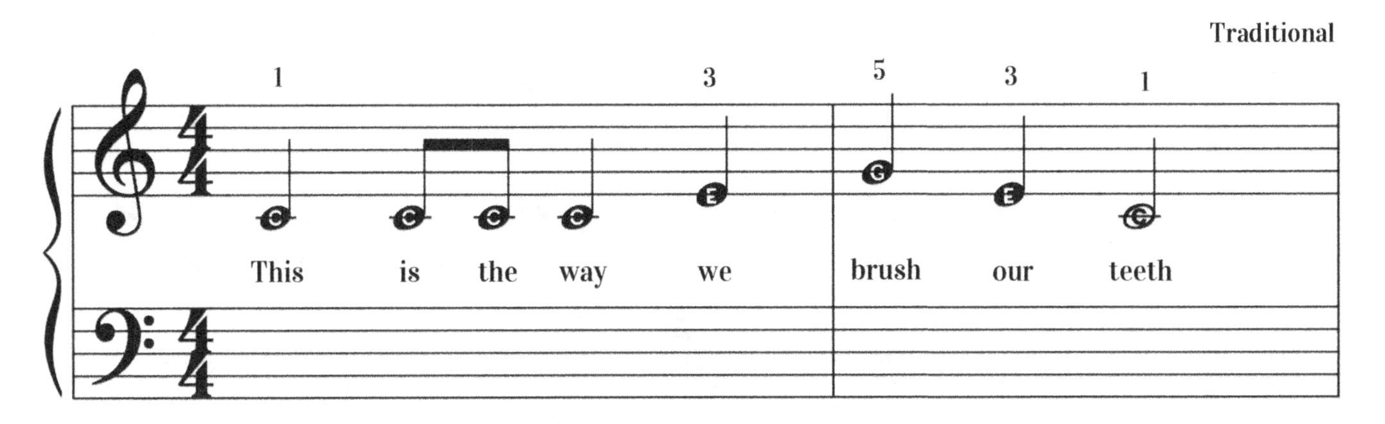

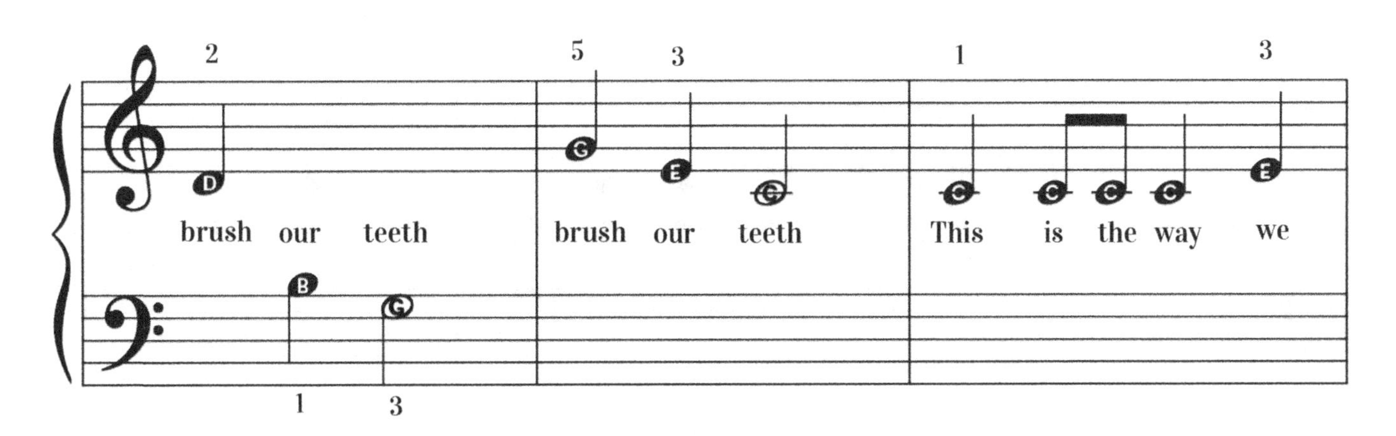

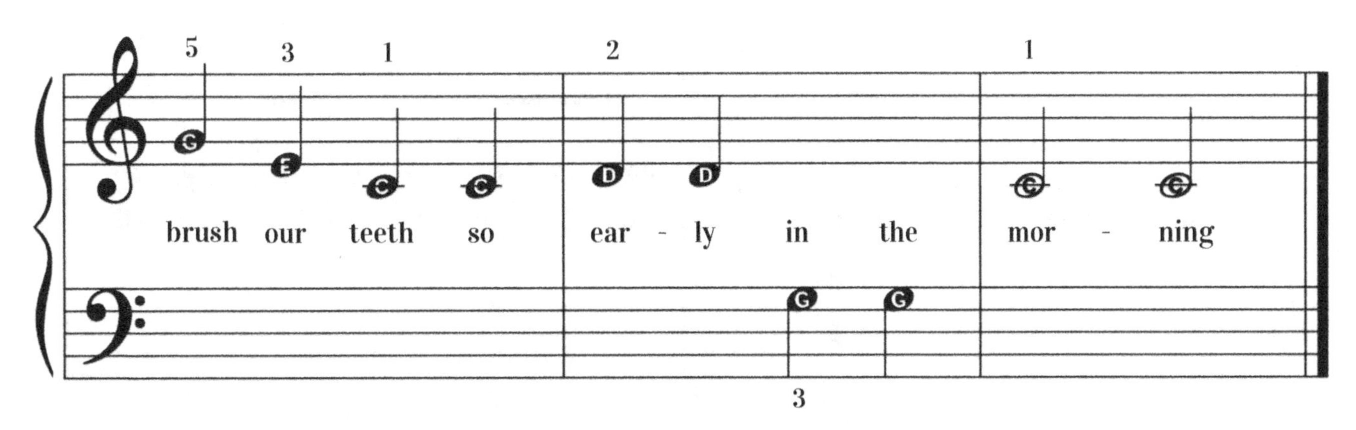

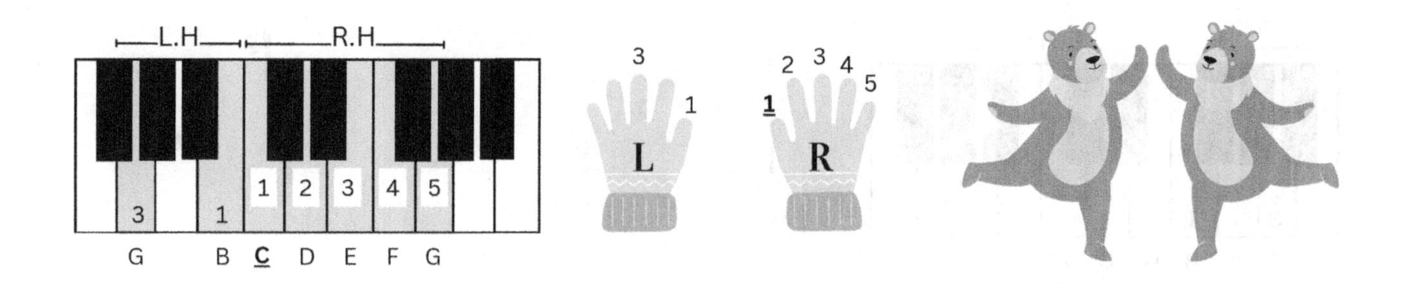

A Ram Sam Sam

Traditional

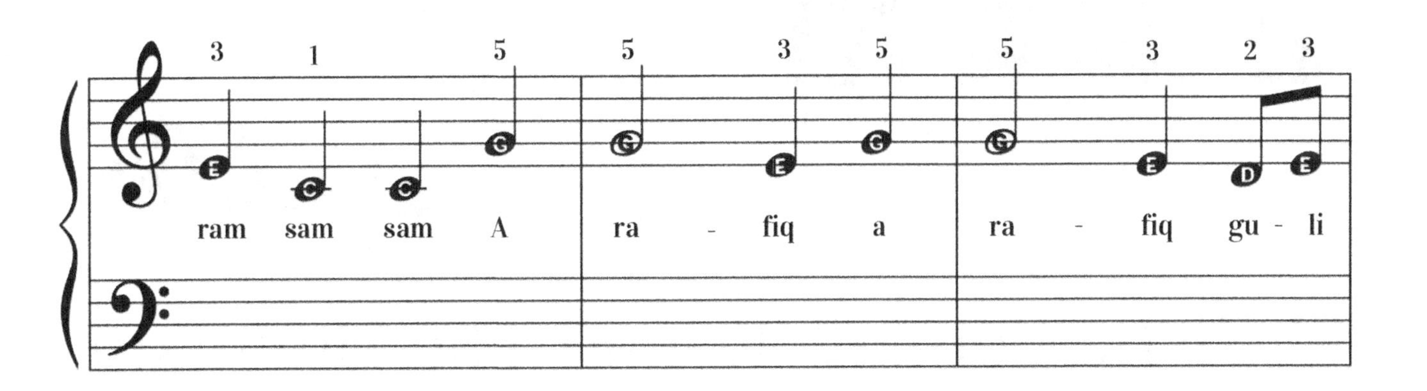

Do you know that "A Ram Sam Sam" is a traditional Moroccan children's song? It features some nonsensical words, but "a rafiq" means "friend" and "guli" means "tell me."

Nonsensical words? Great! Even a dog might understand this one!

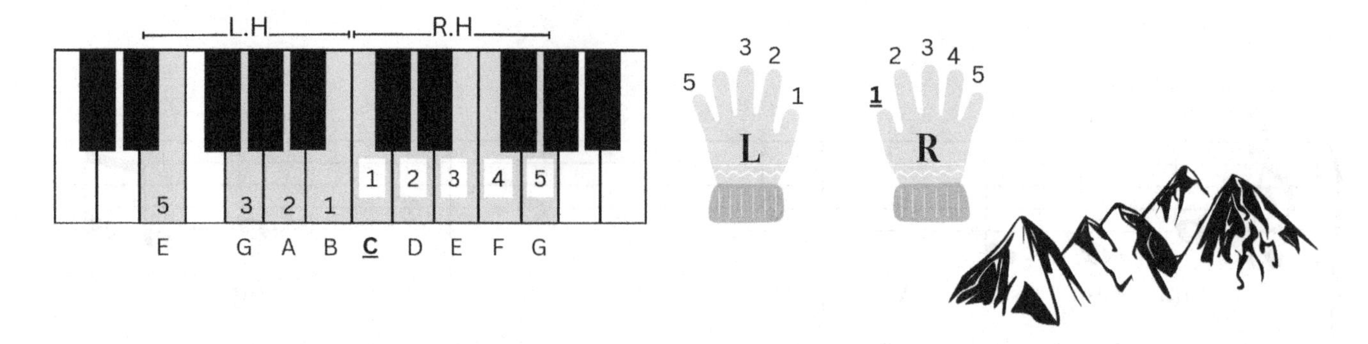

She'll Be Coming 'Round The Mountain

Traditional

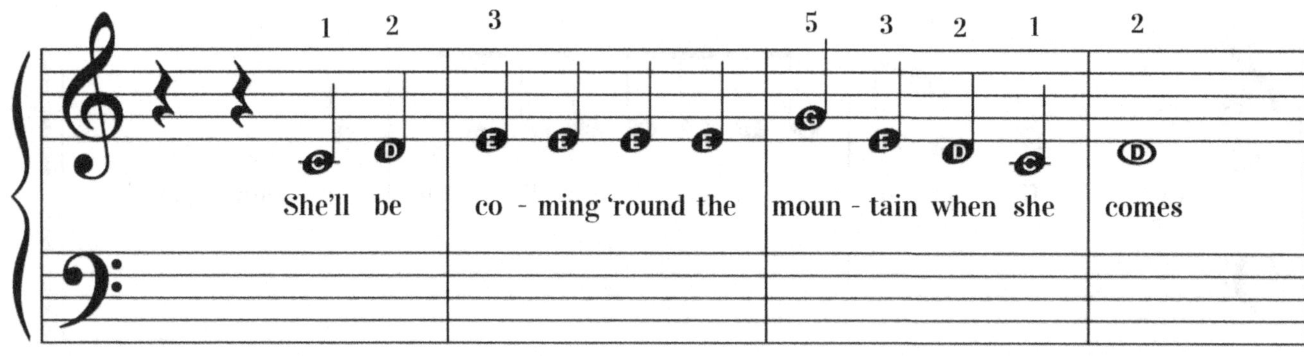

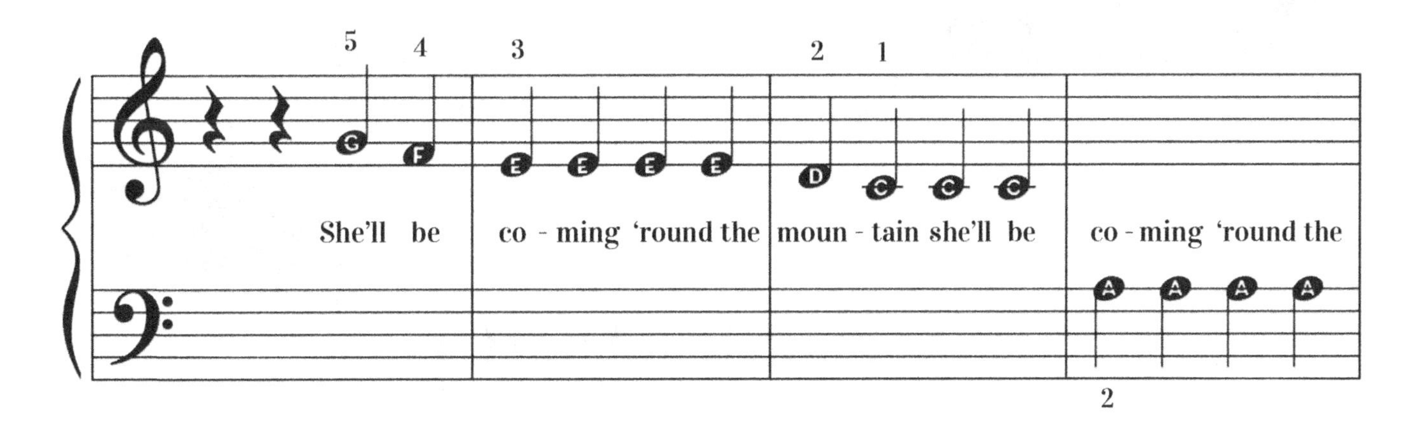
5 4 3 2 1
She'll be co - ming 'round the moun - tain she'll be co - ming 'round the
2

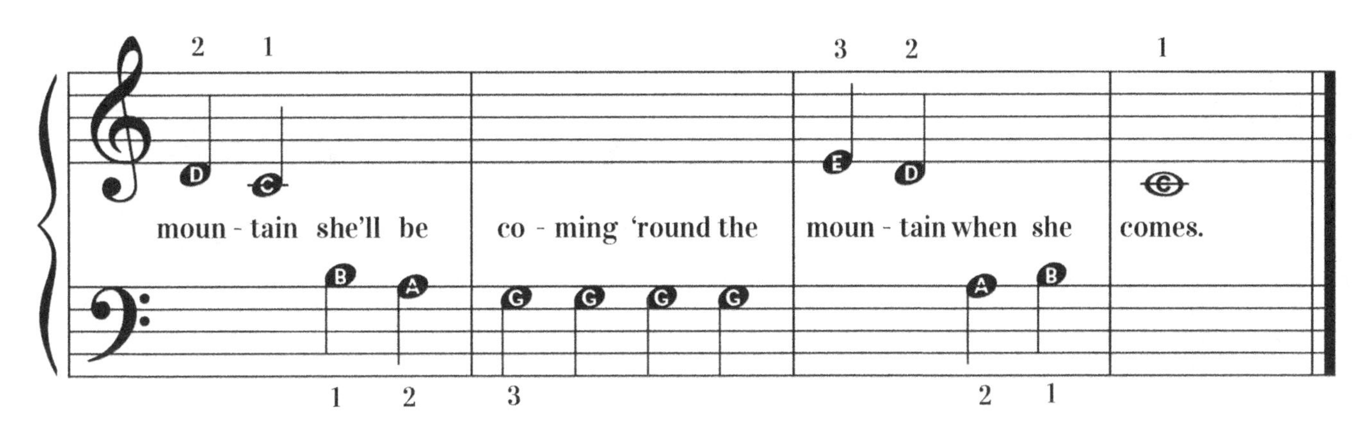
2 1 3 2 1
moun - tain she'll be co - ming 'round the moun - tain when she comes.
1 2 3 2 1

Look! This must be a trap for human!

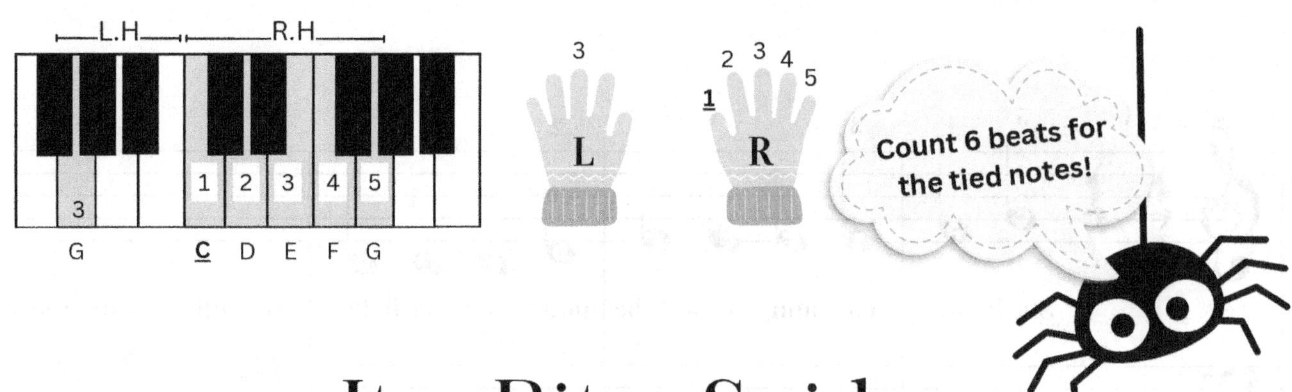

Itsy Bitsy Spider

Traditional

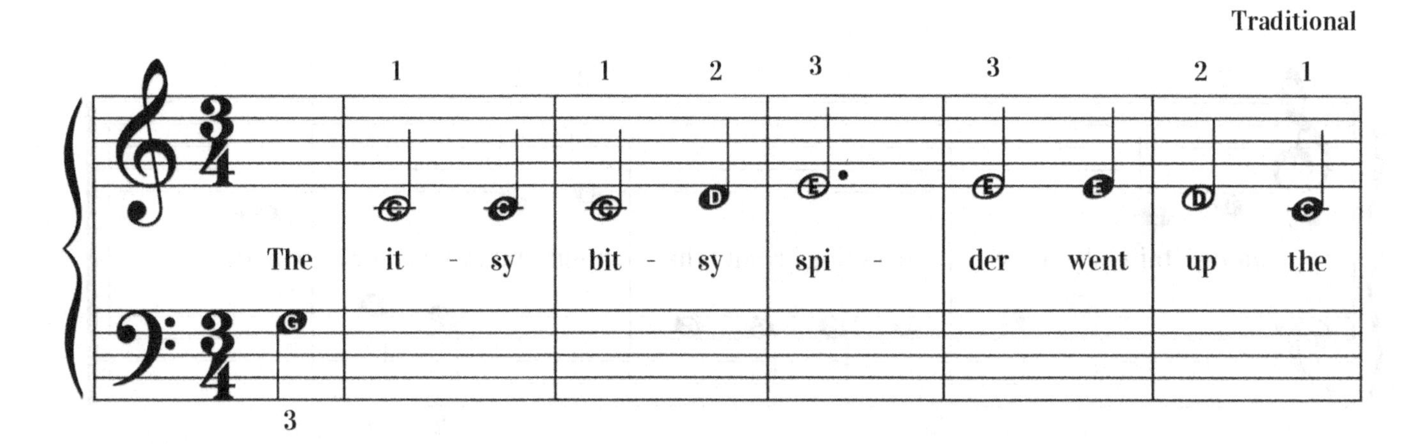

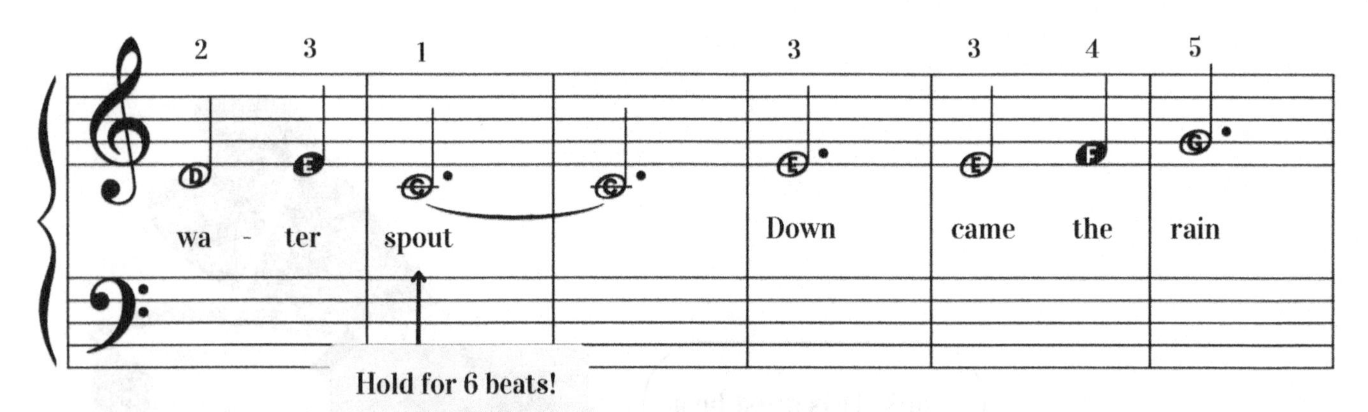

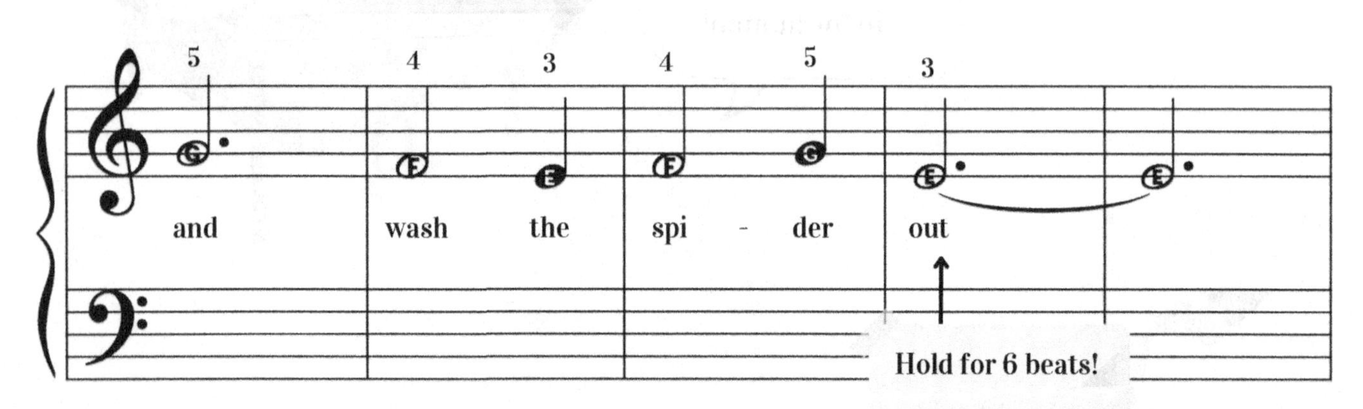

A tie is a curved line connecting two or more notes of the same pitch..
It joins their time values together so that they are played as if they were one note!

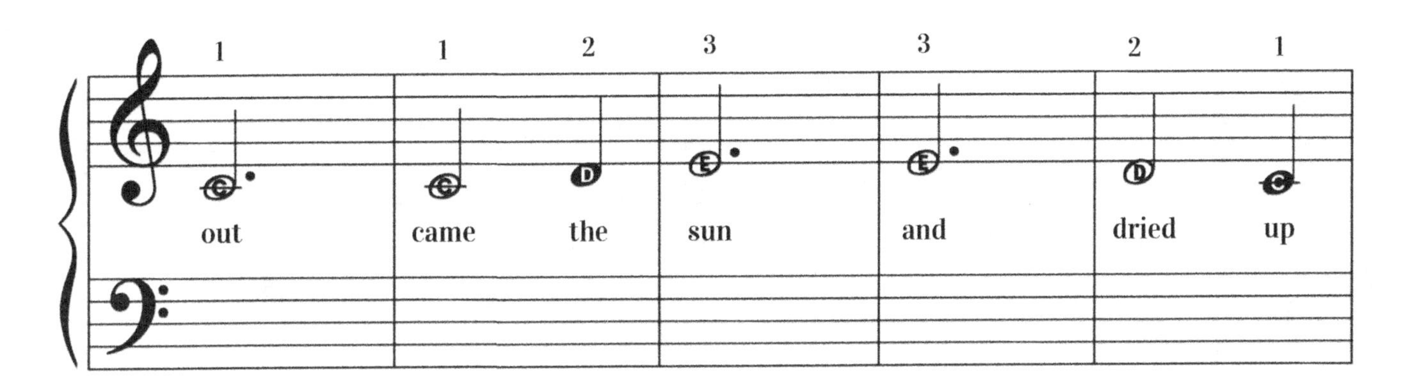
1
1
2
3
3
2
1
C
C
D
E
E
D
C
out
came
the
sun
and
dried
up

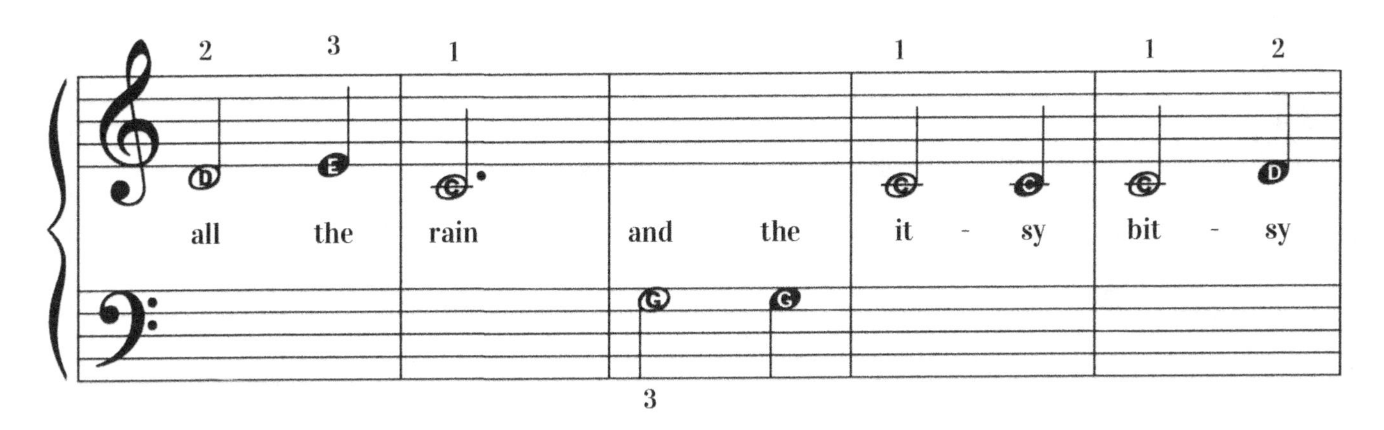
2
3
1
1
1
2
D
E
C
C
C
C
D
all
the
rain
and
the
it - sy
bit - sy
G
G
3

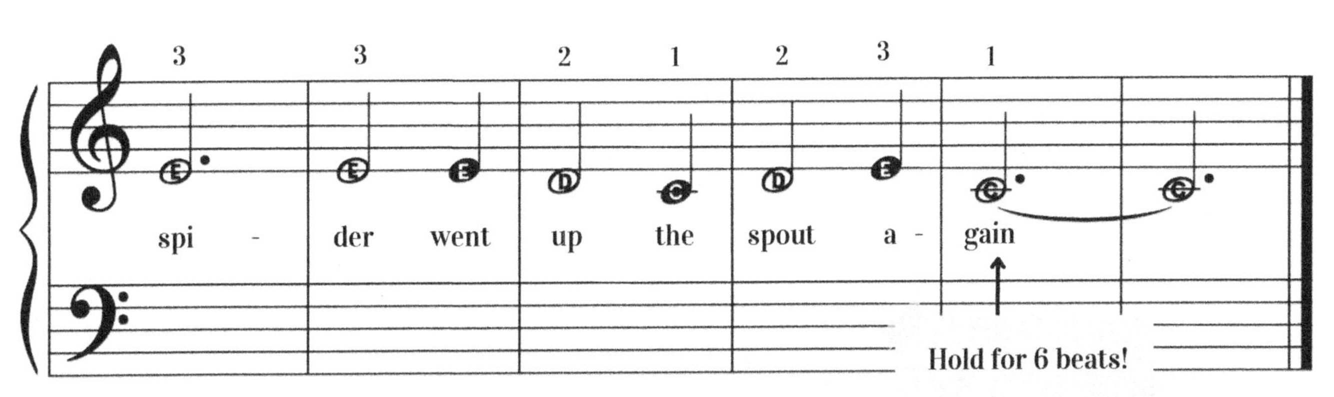
3
3
2
1
2
3
1
E
E
E
D
C
D
E
C
C
spi -
der
went
up
the
spout
a -
gain
Hold for 6 beats!

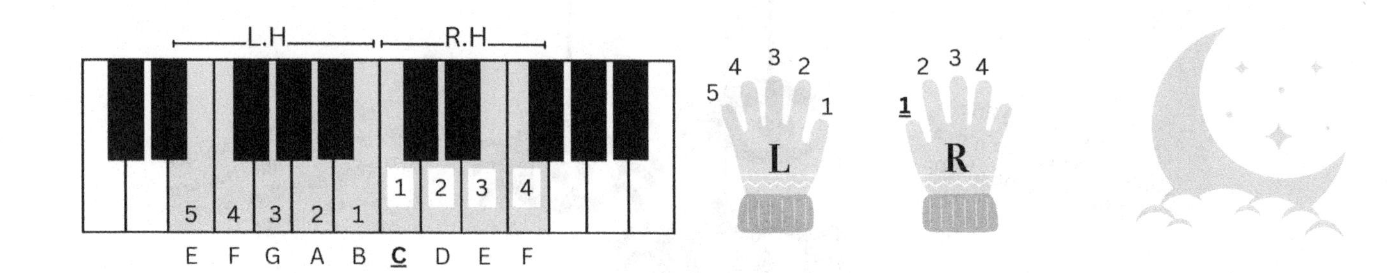

Rock-A-Bye Baby

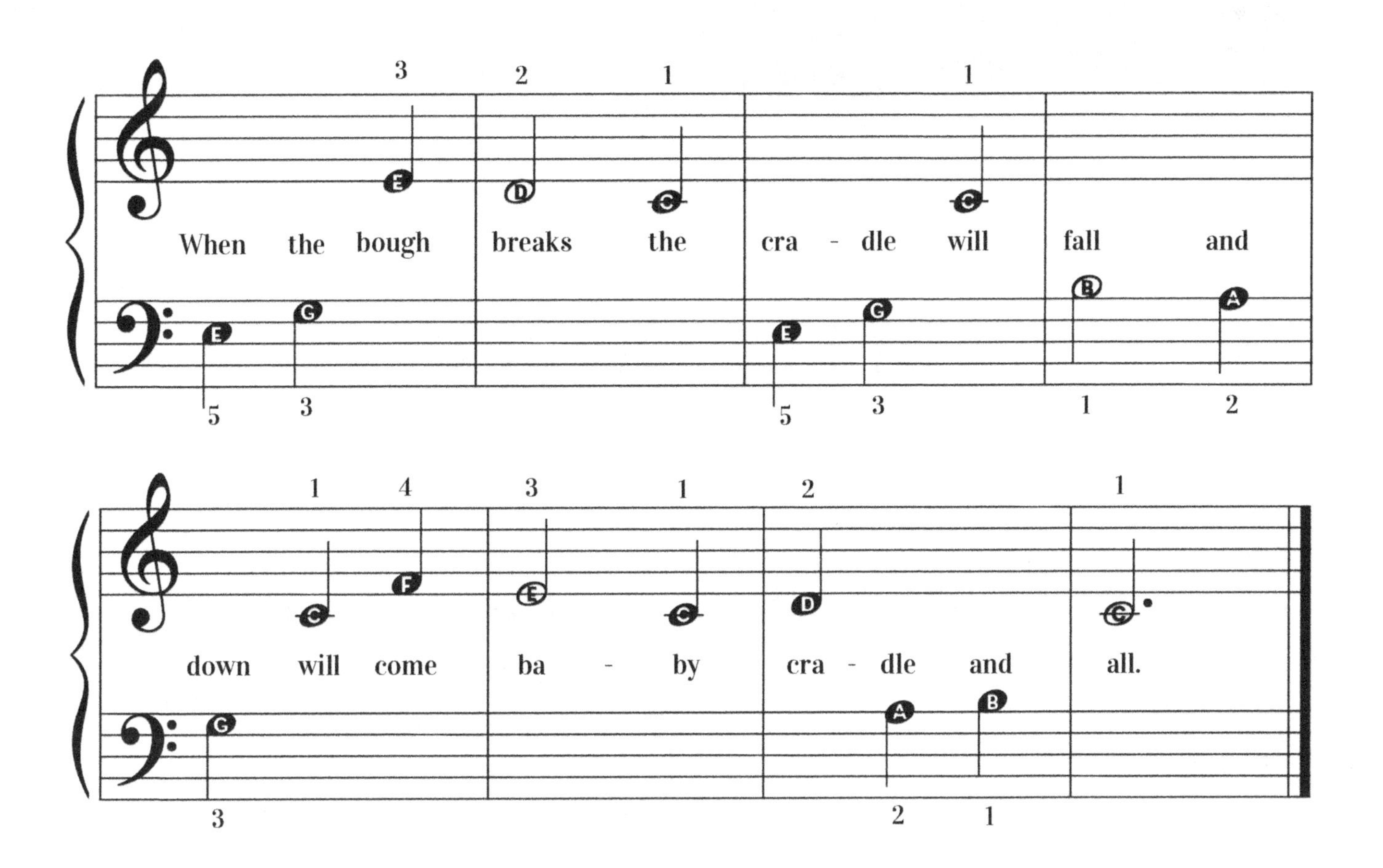
When the bough breaks the cra - dle will fall and
down will come ba - by cra - dle and all.

Why did the piano teacher bring a ladder to class?
Because she wanted to reach the high notes!

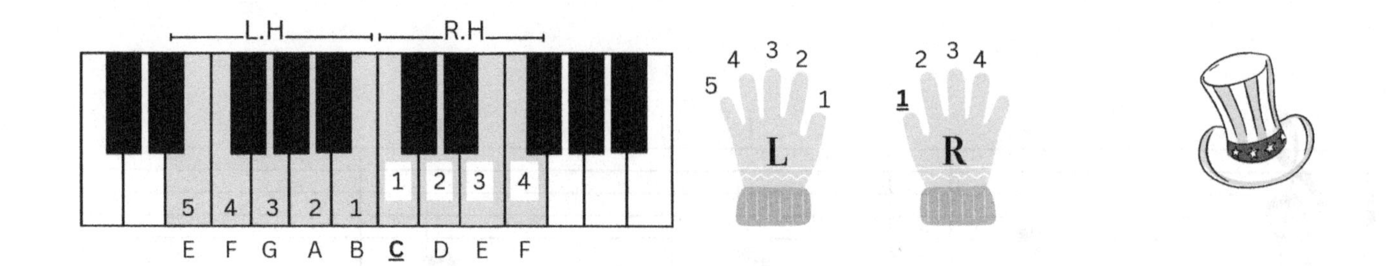

Yankee Doodle

Traditional

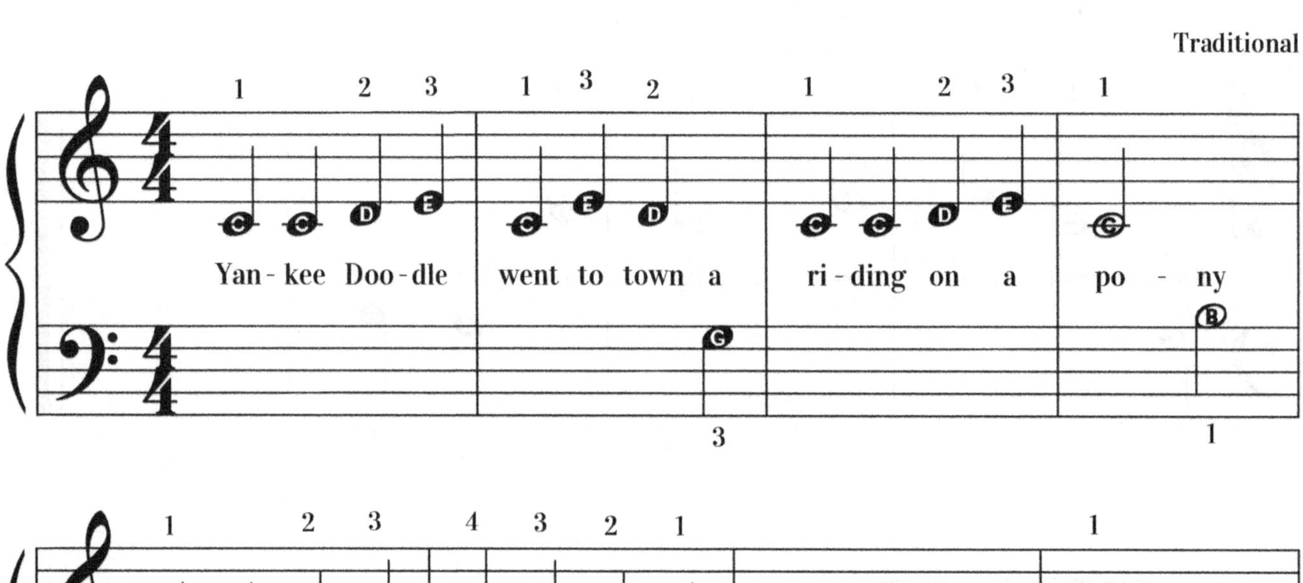

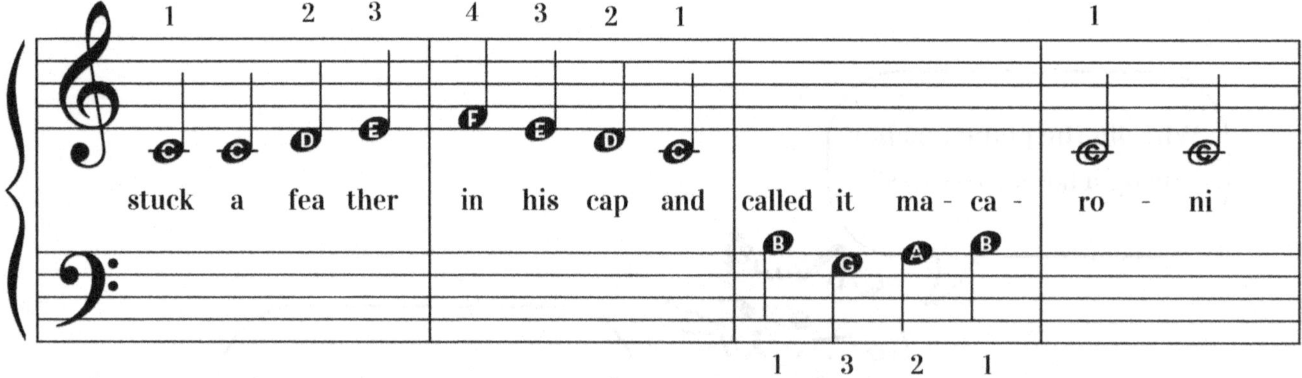

Yan - kee Doo - dle keep it up! Yan - kee Doo - dle dan - dy,
mind the mu - sic and the step and with the girls be han - dy!

Do you know "macaroni" in "Yankee Doddle" isn't talking about Mac n Cheese? It means someone was dressing super fancy, like putting a feather in your cap and calling it stylish!
Huh? Macaroni on your hat? I'll stick to eating mine, thank you very much!

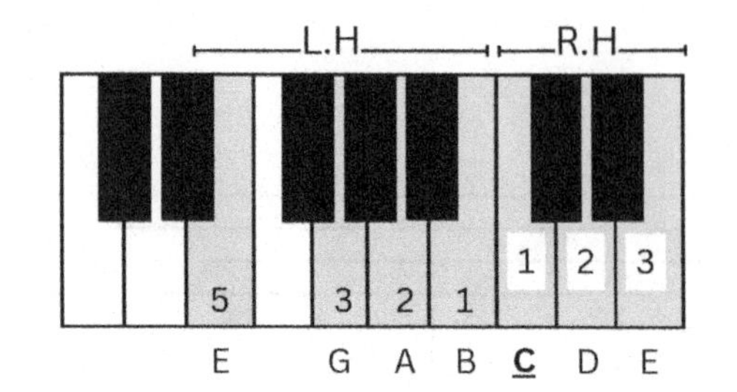

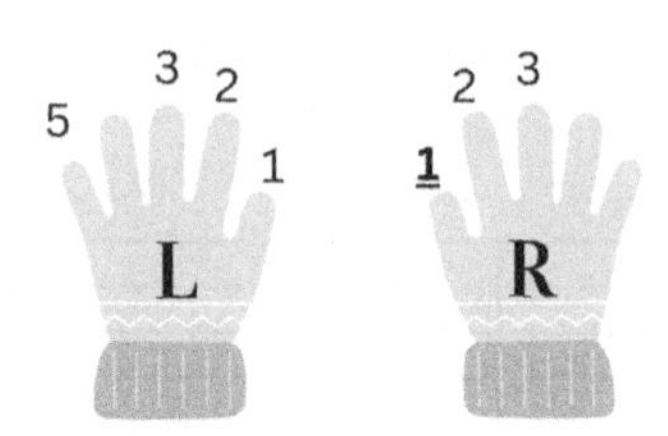

My Bonnie Lies Over The Ocean

Traditional

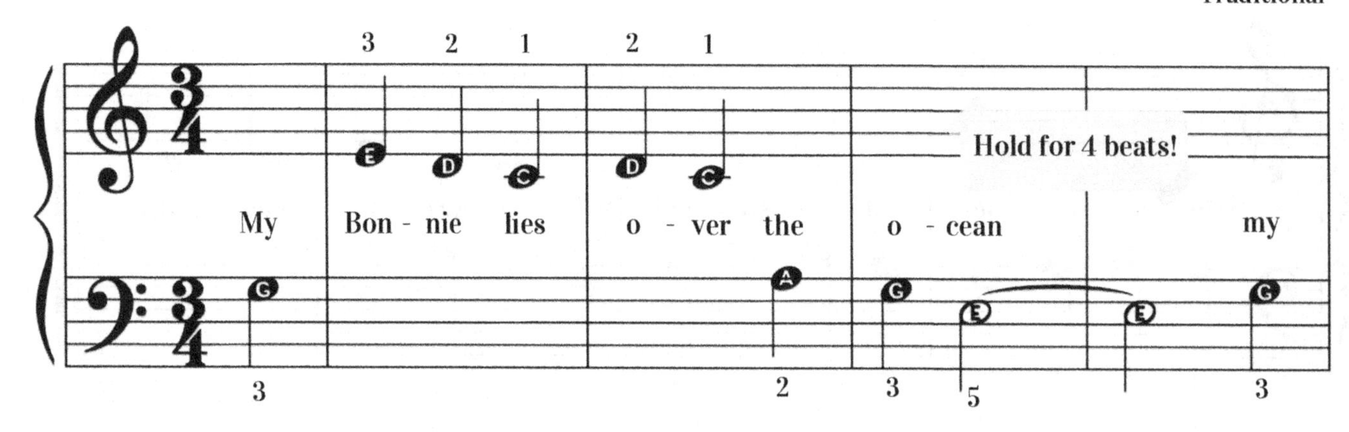

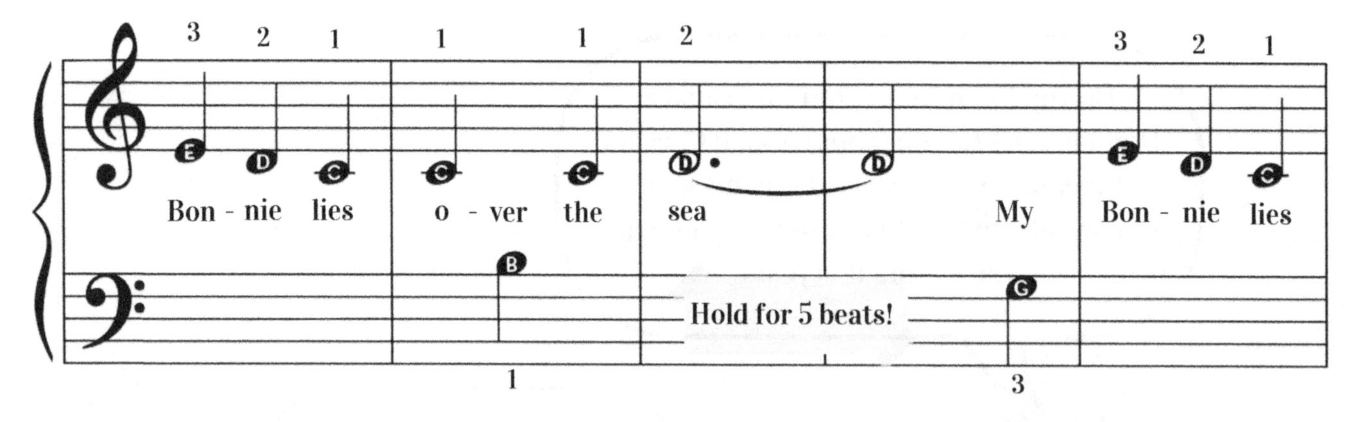

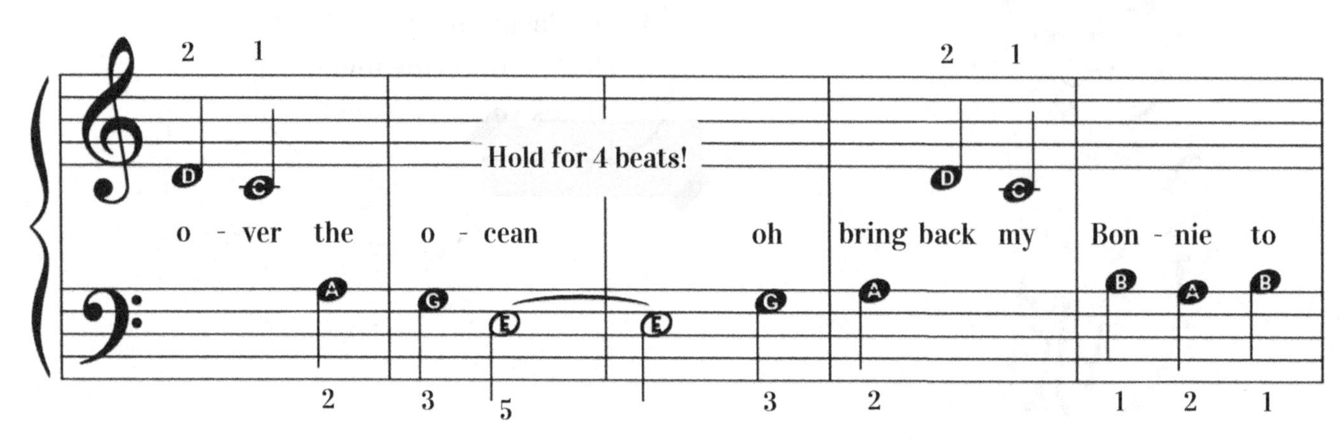

Hold for 6 beats!

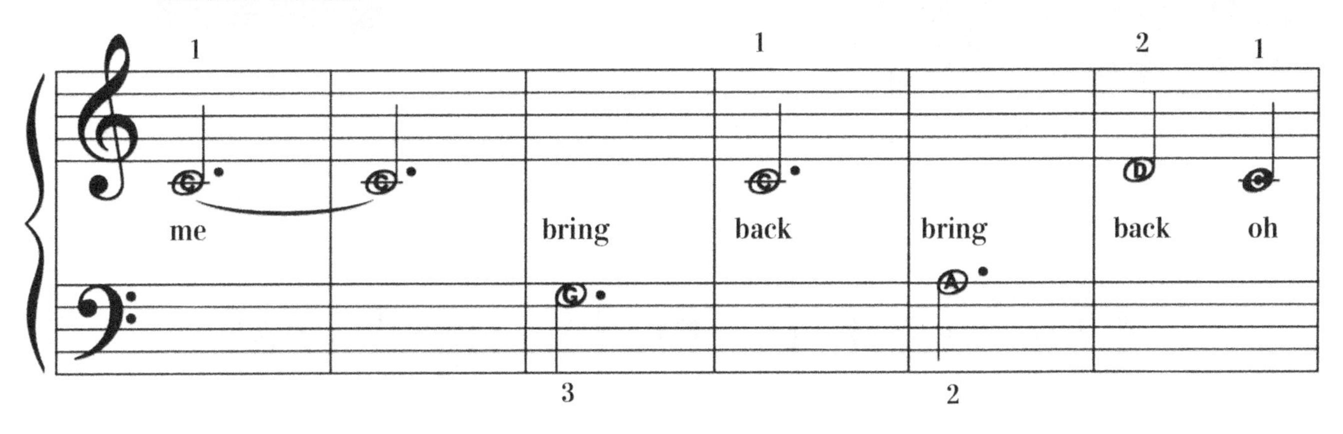

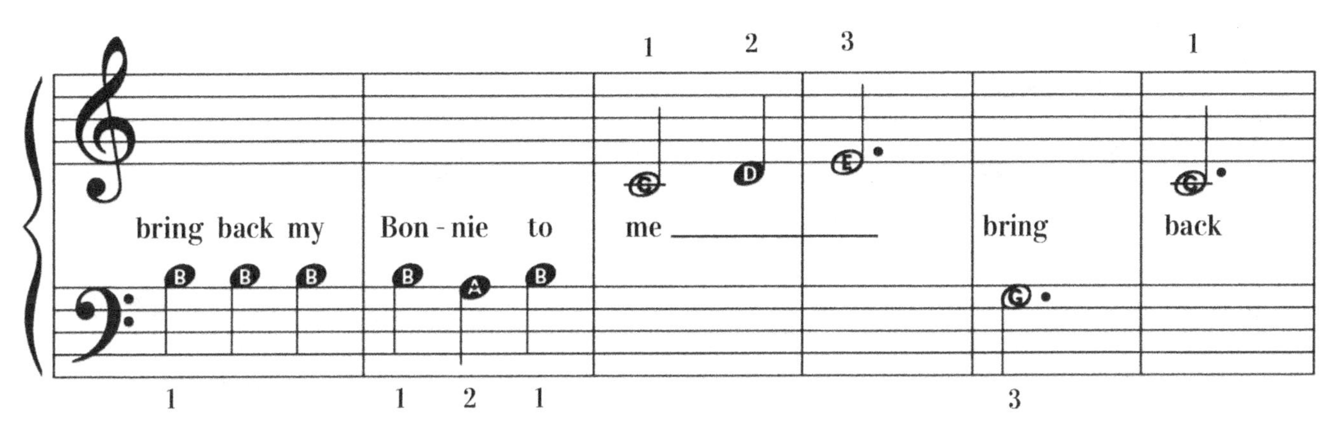

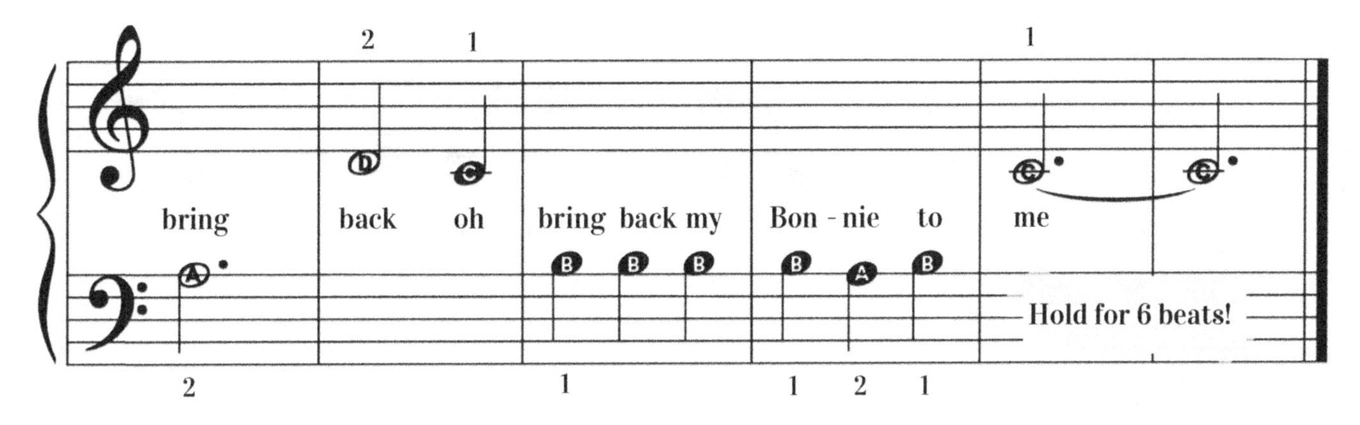

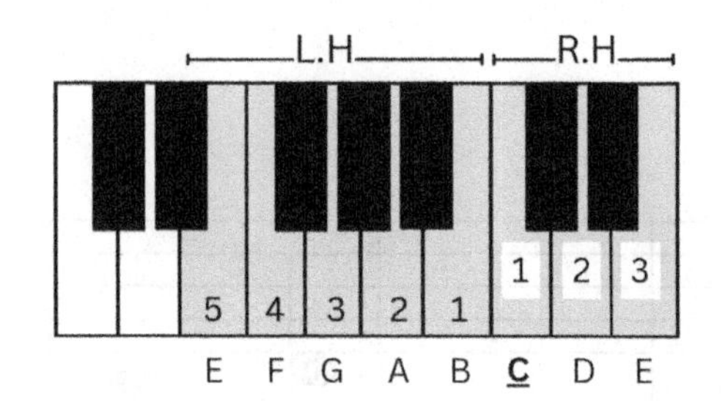

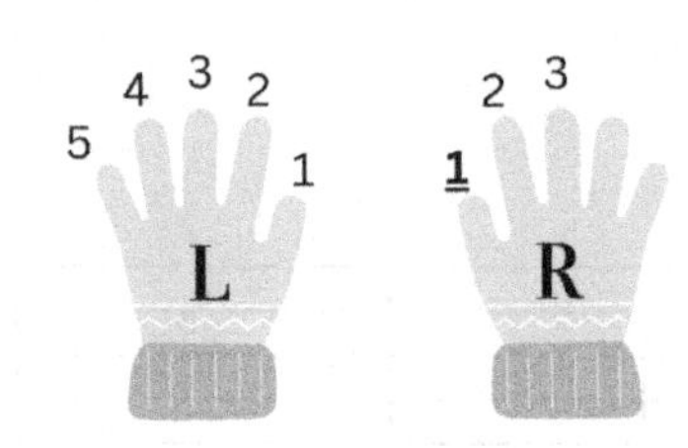

Do Your Ears Hang Low

Traditional

3 2 2 1 2 3 2 1
E D D C D E D C C C C C
tie 'em in a bow? Can you throw 'em o'er your shoul - der like a
G E F
3 5 4
1 2 3 2 1
C D E D C
con- ti - nen - tal sol -dier? Do your ears hang low?
G A G E G G
3 2 3 5 3 3

How did the piano get out of jail?
With its keys!

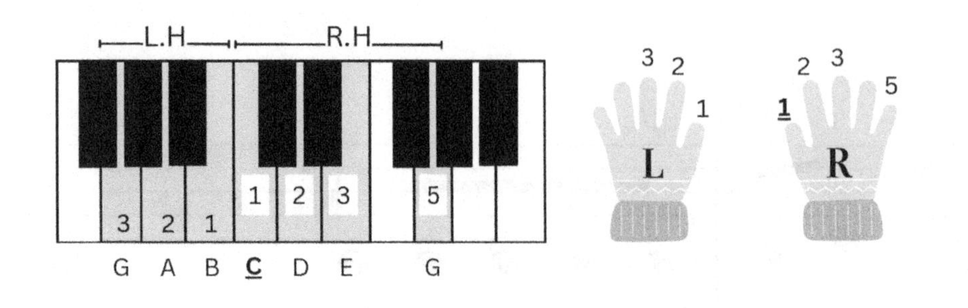

Camptown Races

Stephen Foster

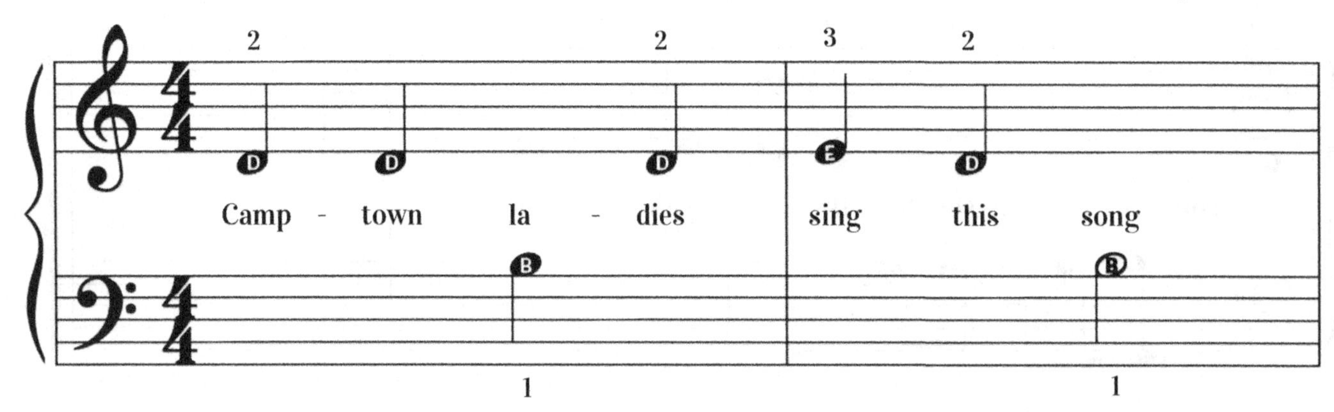

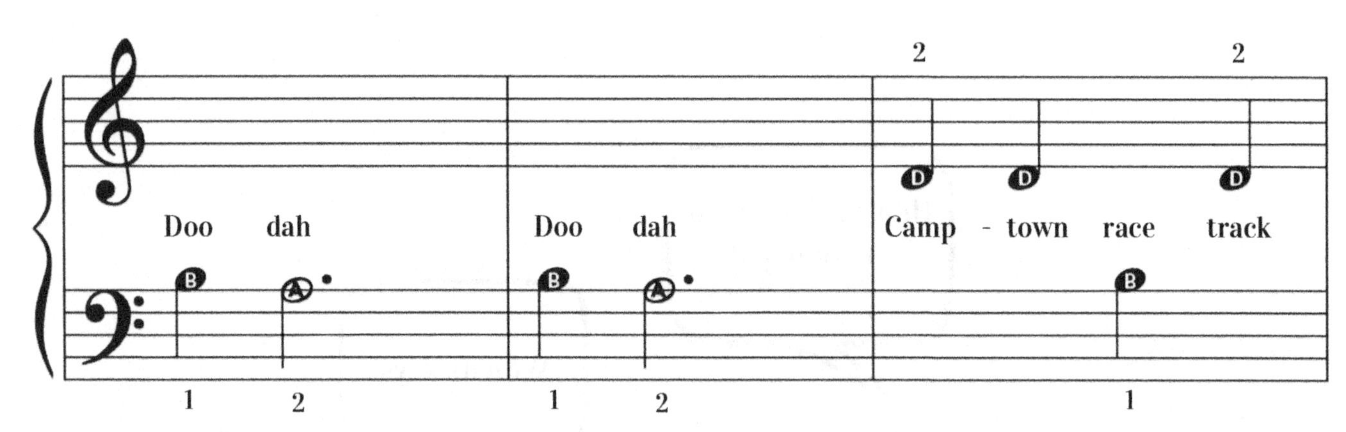

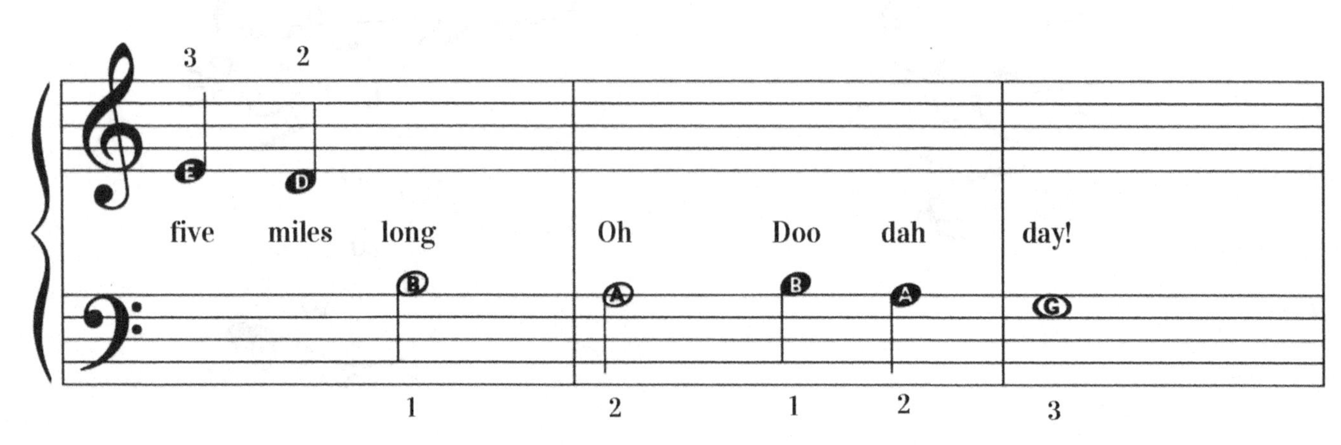

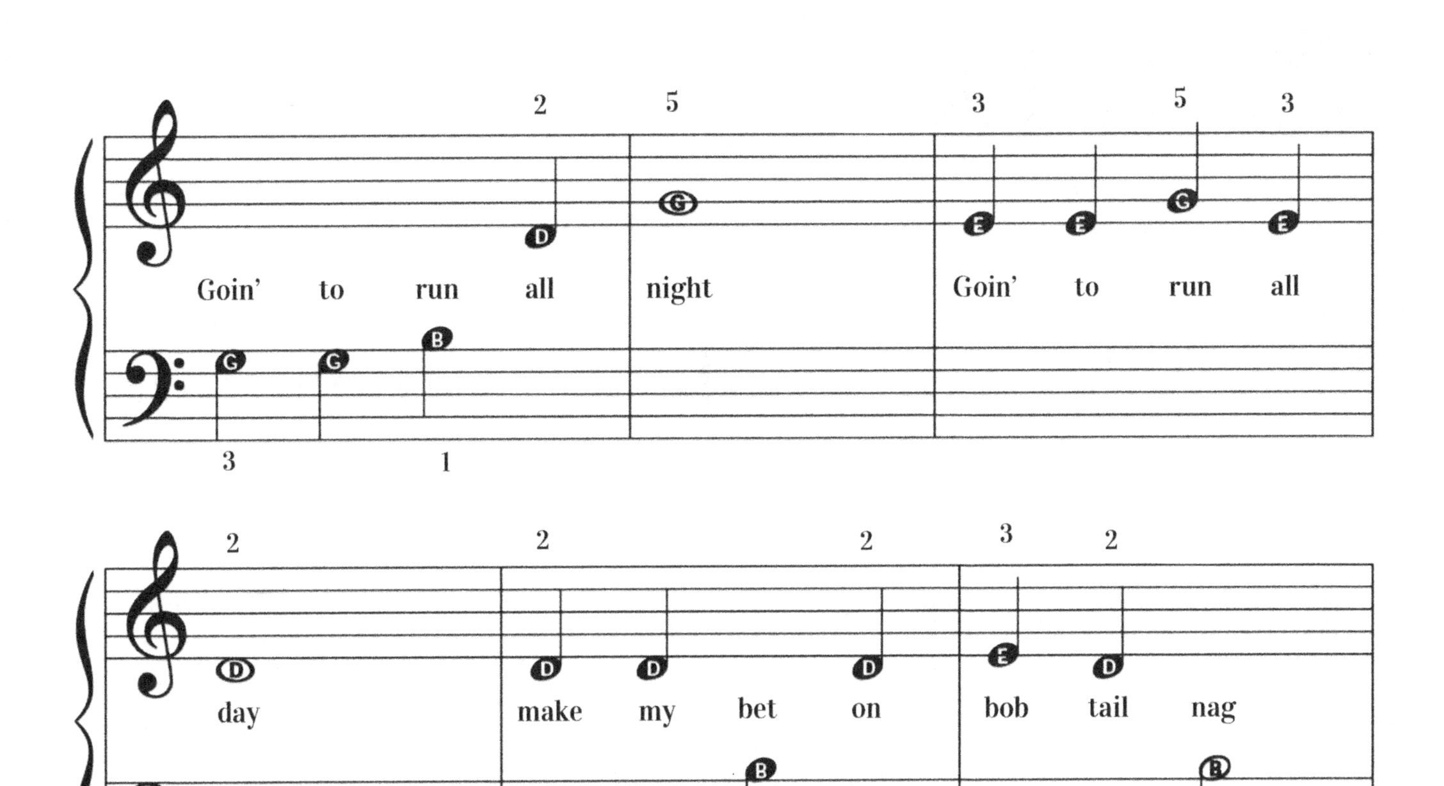
Goin' to run all night
Goin' to run all day
make my bet on bob tail nag

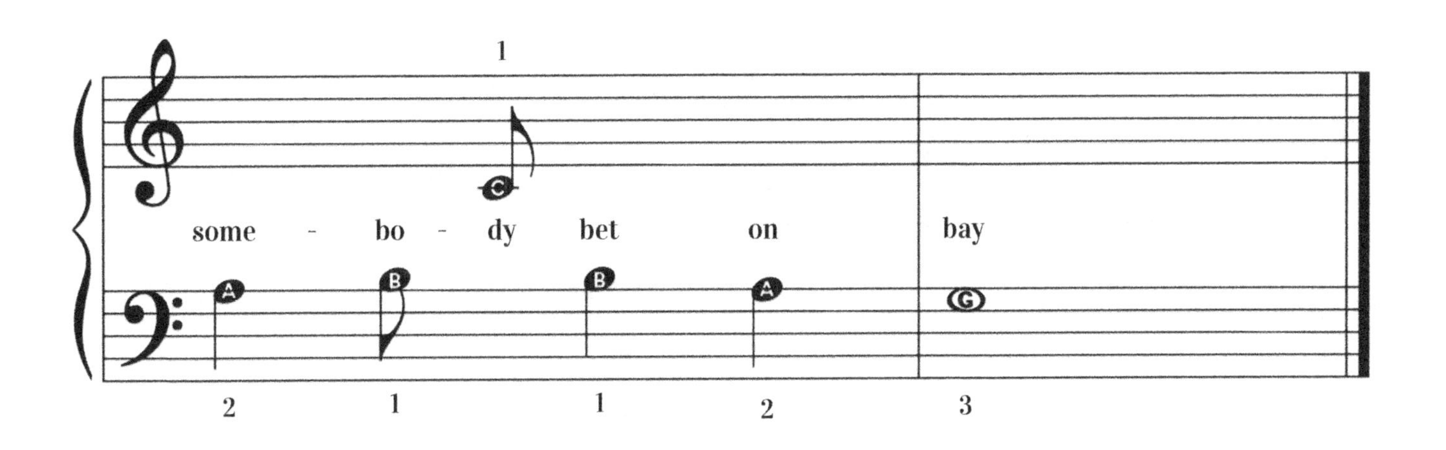
some - bo - dy bet on bay

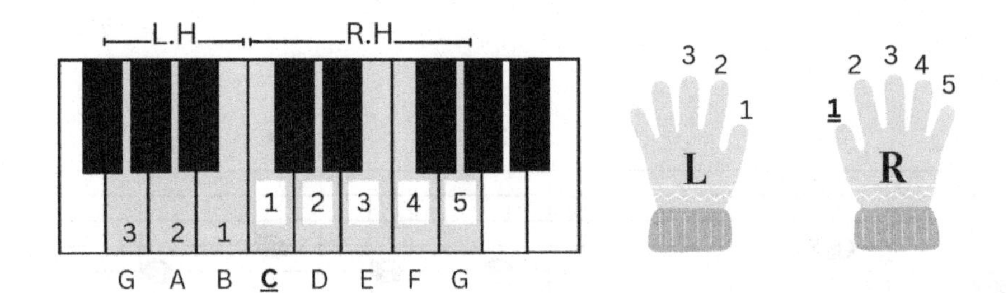

We Wish You A Merry Christmas

Traditional

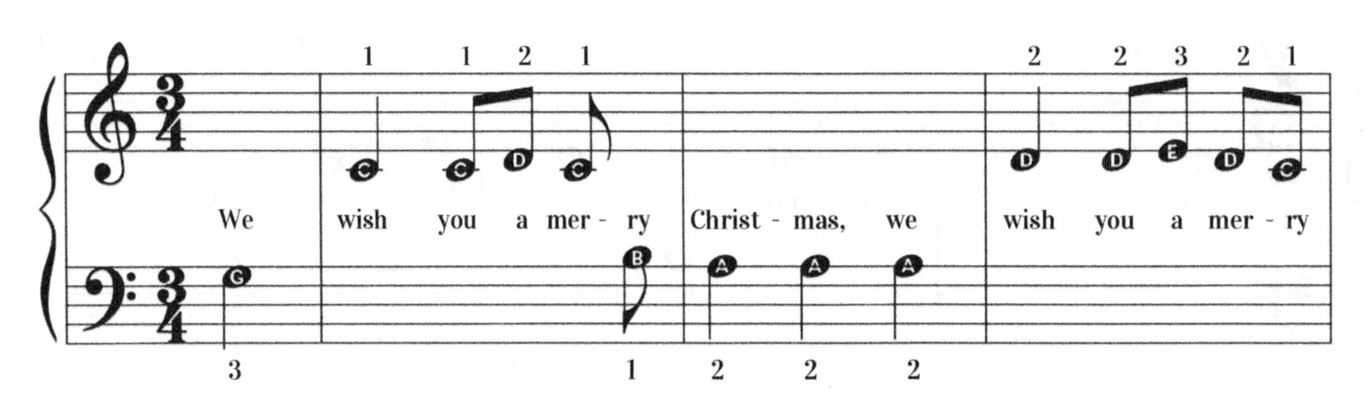

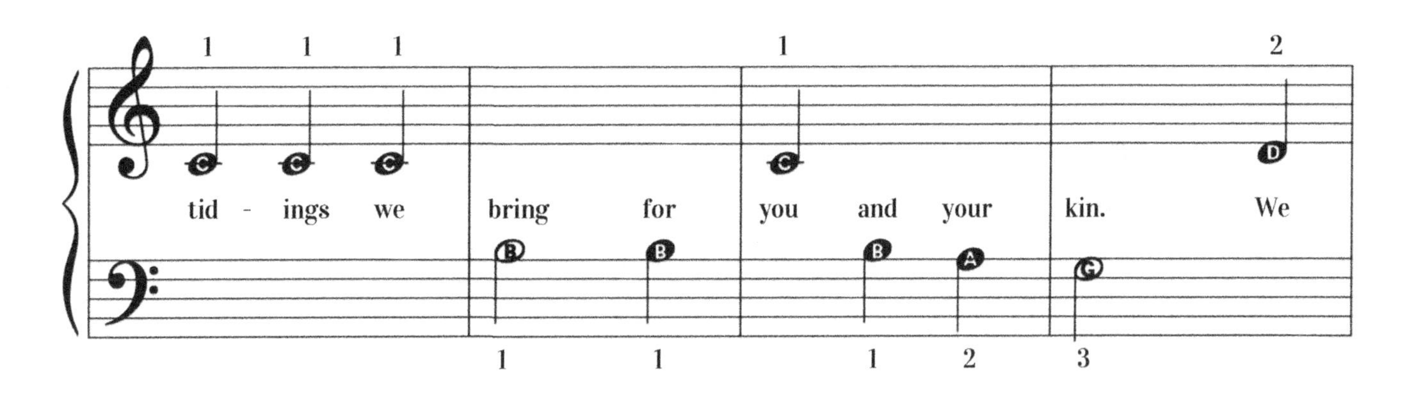
1 1 1 1 2
C C C C D
tid - ings we bring for you and your kin. We
B B B A G
1 1 1 2 3

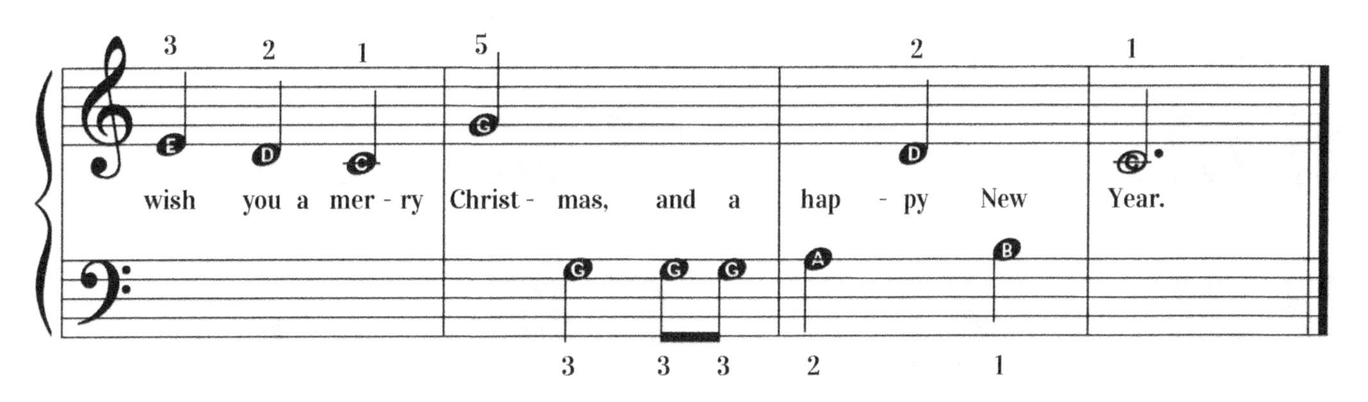
3 2 1 5 2 1
E D C G D C
wish you a mer - ry Christ - mas, and a hap - py New Year.
G G G A B
3 3 3 2 1

Chapter 3

All songs in this chapter are written in the following hand position, so let's get familiar with it!

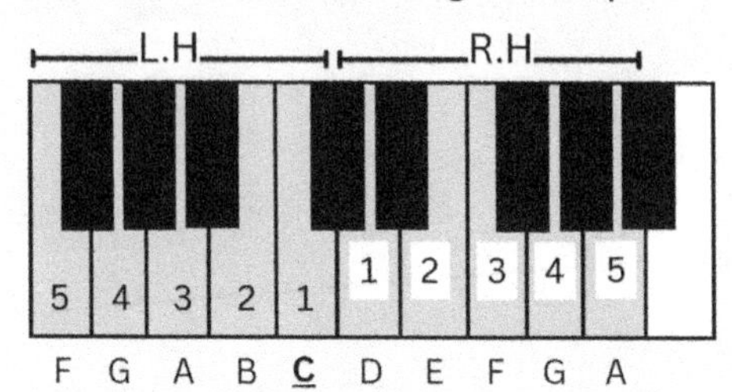

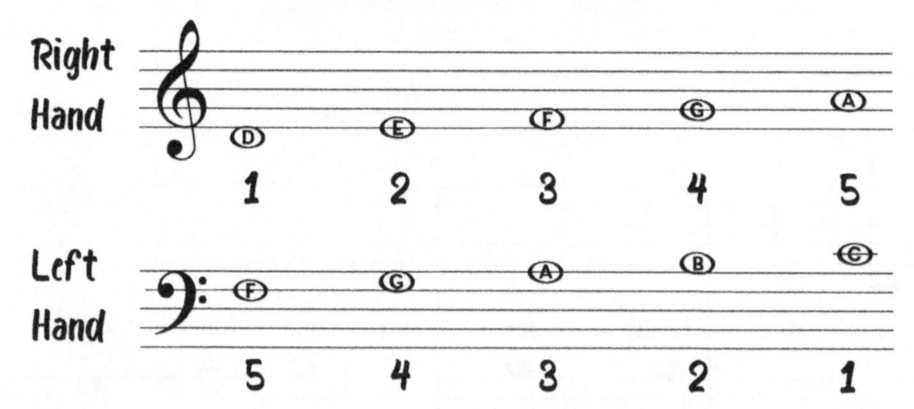

Name the notes and connect it to the right keys! The first one is done for you.

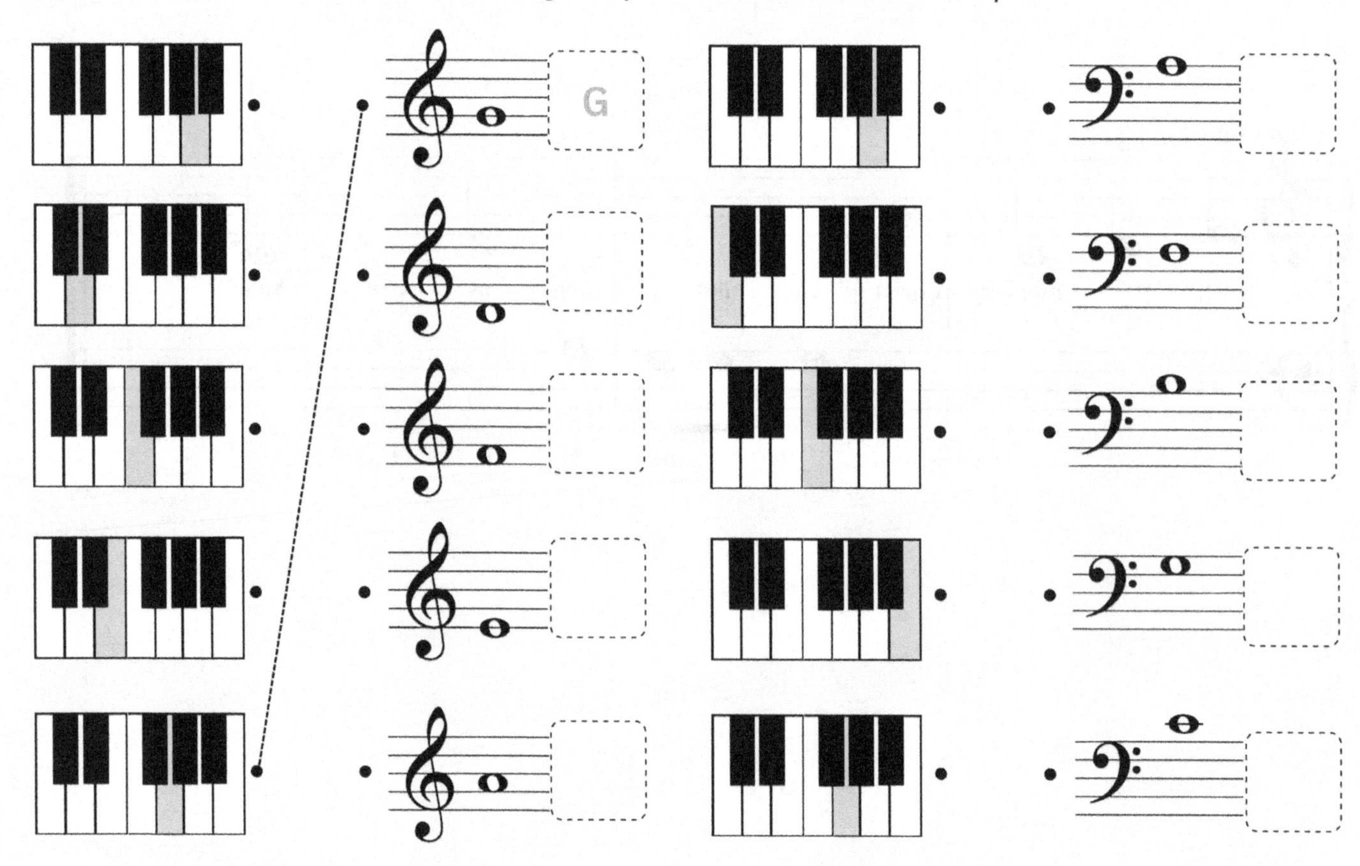

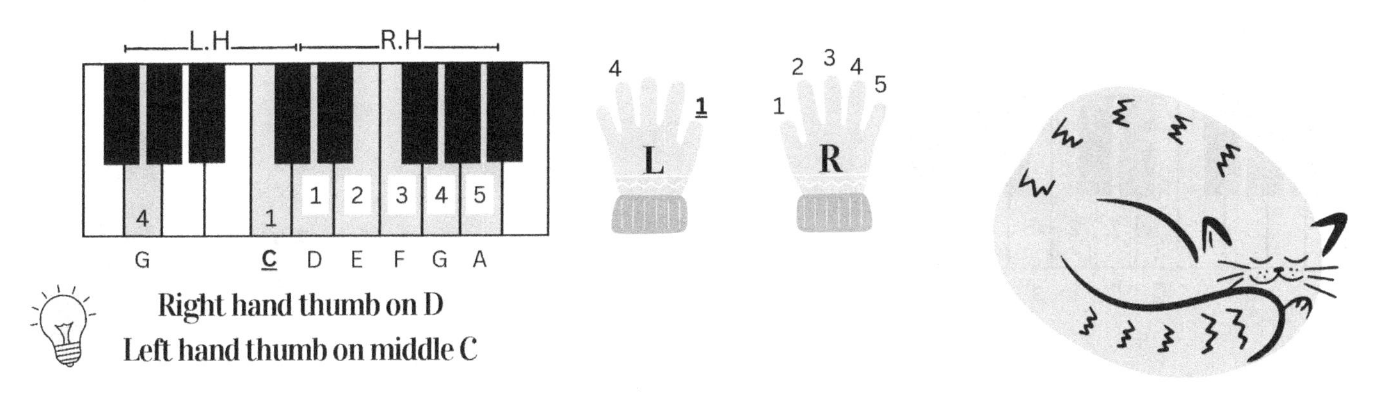

Are You Sleeping

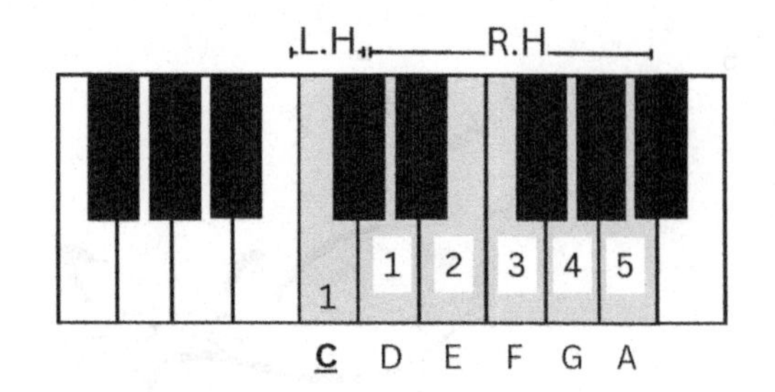

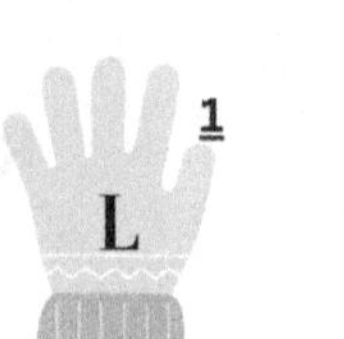

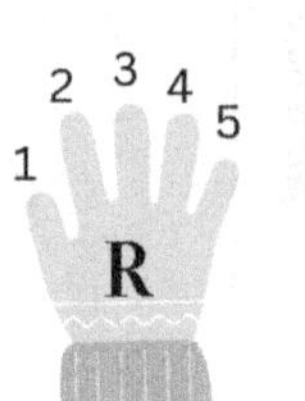

This Old Man

Traditional

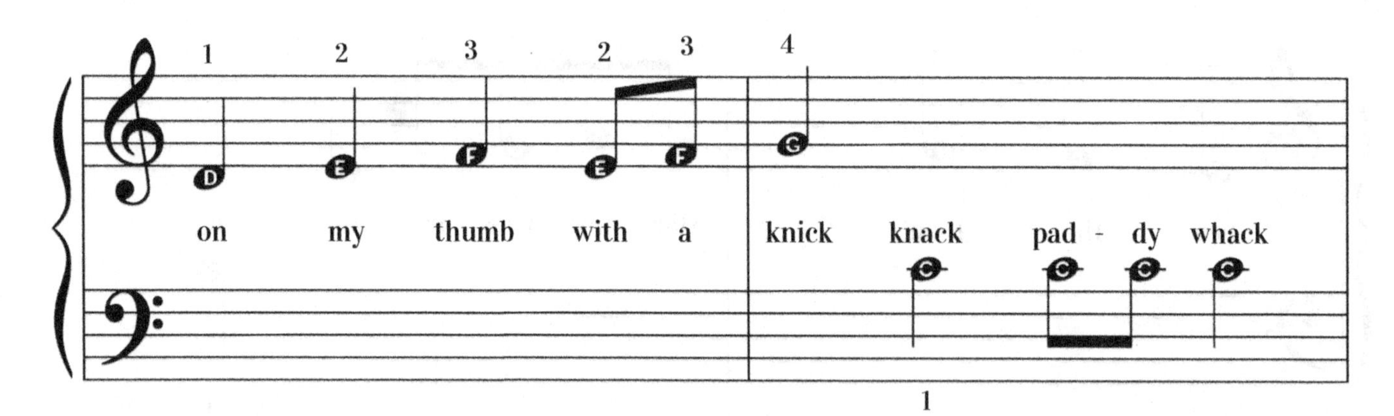

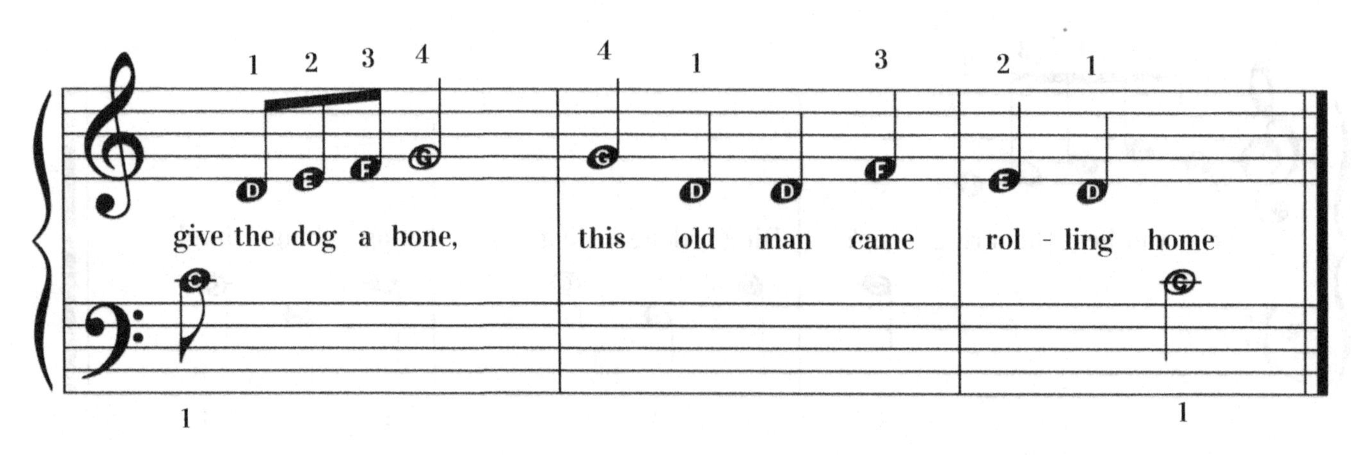

Name each key and reveal the secret code! The first one is done for you.

The Spy enter the C A F E for a meeting.

The suspect with a long ____ ____ ____ ____ waited nervously.

We must open the ____ ____ ____ ____ after the signal.

The diamond is hidden in the ____ ____ ____

Next to the sparkling ____ ____ ____ ____

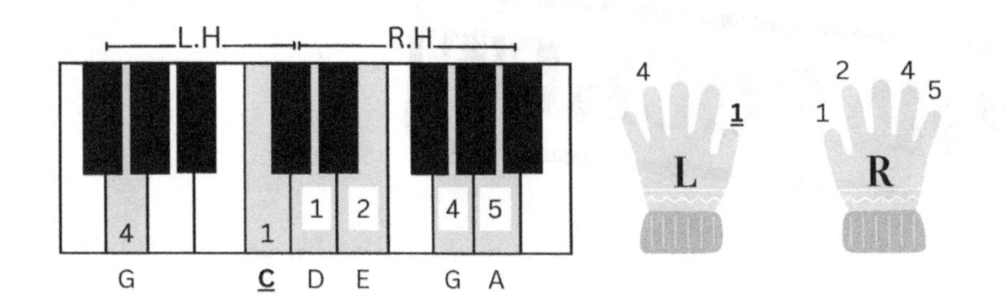

The Farmer In The Dell

Traditional

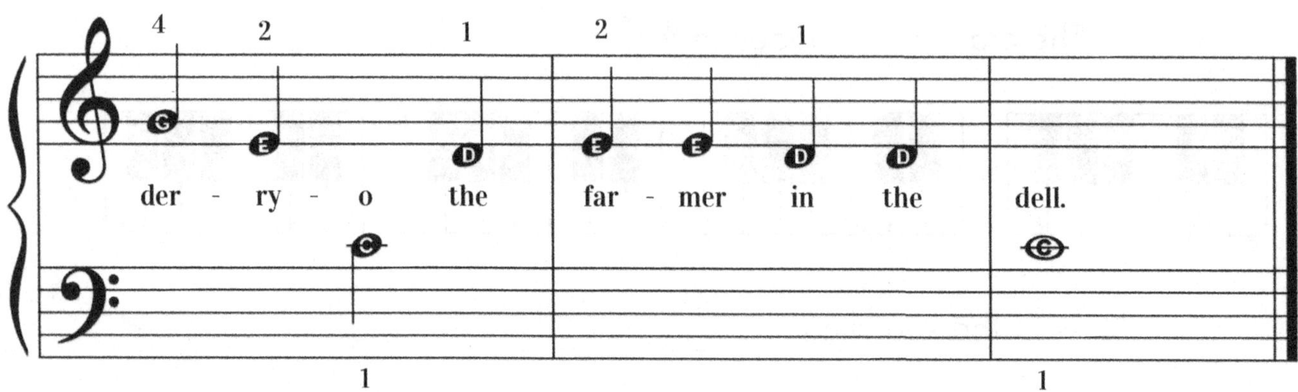

Use your spy skills and musical knowledge to locate the hidden music notes in the word search. They could be hidden horizontal or vertical. The first one is done for you.

Bb	E	C	A#	G	C#	D
C	C	D	Eb	G	C	C
F	A	G	B	F	D	F
Bb	B	Gb	F	A	A	E
A	G	A	B	D	E	A
G	C	D#	C	A	C#	B
D	D	G	B	A	G	F

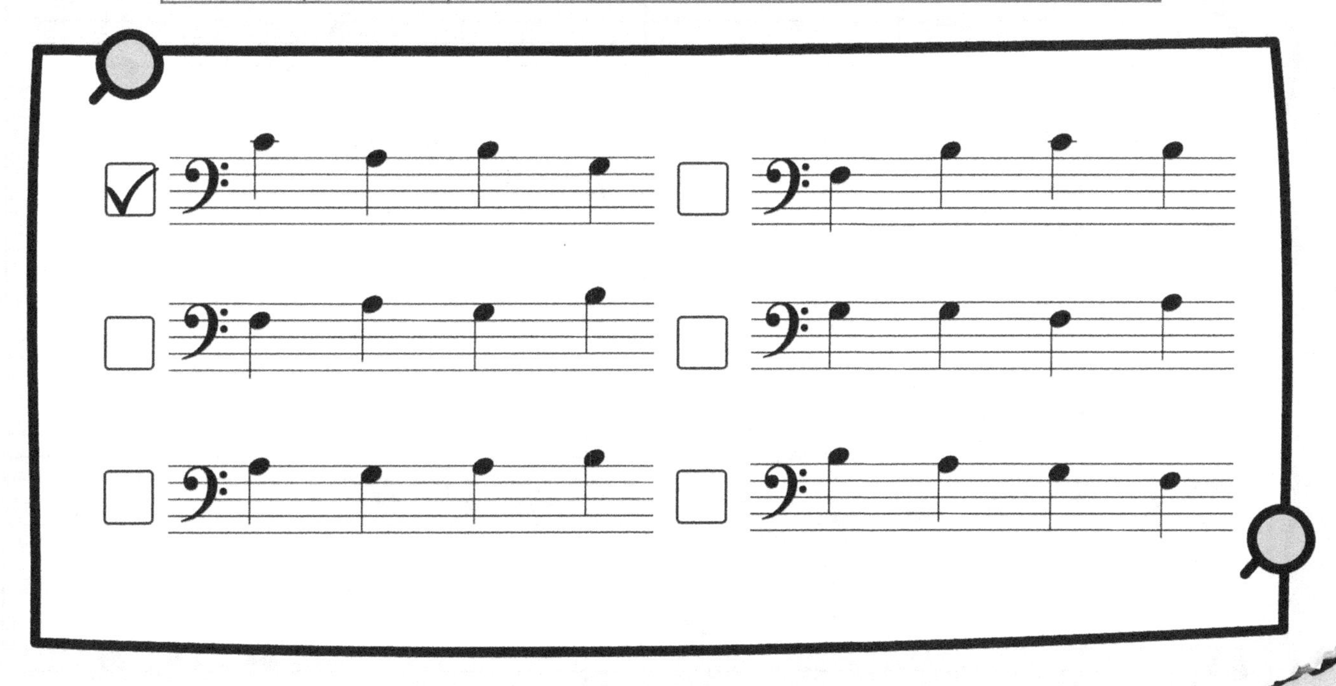

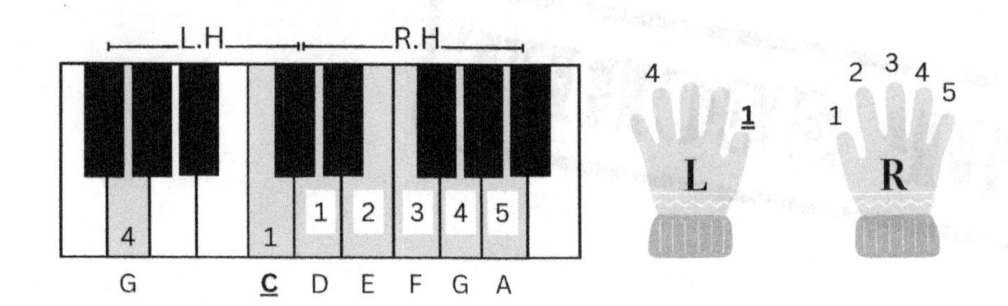
L.H
R.H
4 1 2 3 4 5
G C D E F G A
L
R

Alouette

Traditional
A - lou - et - te gen-tille A - lou-et - te A - lou - et - te
je te plu - me - rai. Je te plu - me - rai la tete
Je te plu - me - rai la tete et la tete et la tete

4
1 2
1 1 2
O!
A - lou - et - te
gen-tille A - lou - et - te
1
1 1 4
1 2 2
1 1 2
A - lou - et - te
je te plu - me - rai.
1
1 1
Yo! Try to clap and count this rhythm pattern before you play the song. It will help you play those dotted quarter notes!
1 n 2 n 3 n 4 n
1 n 2 n 3 n 4 n

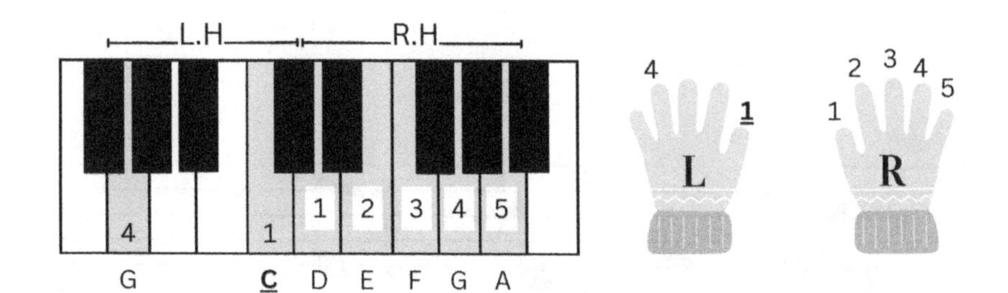

The More We Get Together

Traditional

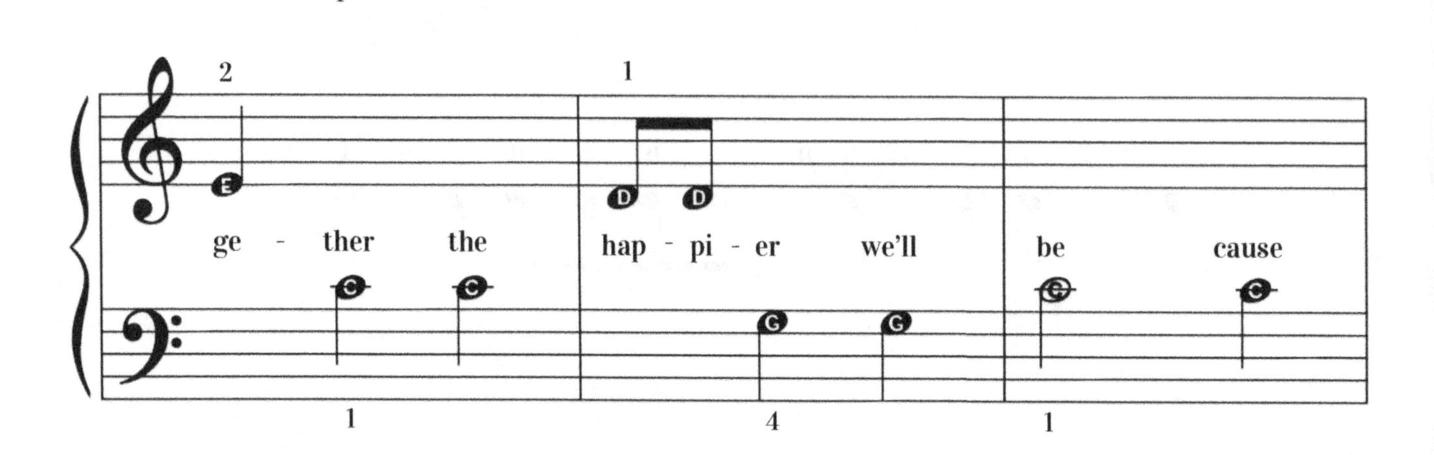

1
2
1
D
E
D
your friends are
my friends and
my friends are
C C
G G
G G
4
1
4
2 2
4 5 4 3
2
E E
G A G F
E
your friends the
more we get to -
ge - ther the
C
C C
1
1
1
D D
hap - pi - er
we'll
be
C
G G
4
1

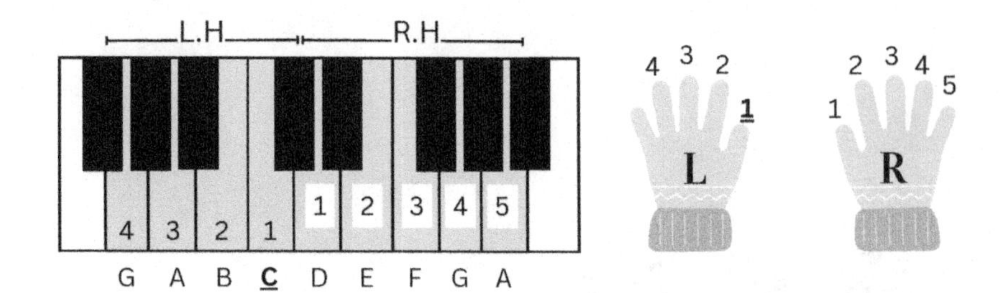

Home On The Range

Daniel E. Kelley

day. Home, home on the range where the
deer and the an - te - lope play. Where sel - dom is heard a dis -
cou - ra - ging word and the skies are not clou - dy all day.

CHapter 4

LET'S PLAY BLACK KEYS

- Imagine you're playing the piano and you see a C note.
- A Sharp sign ♯ means you have to move one step to the **right**, to the very next key which is a black key called C#

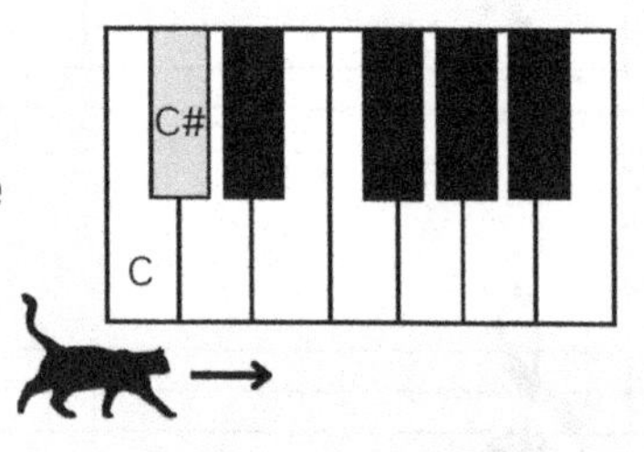

- Imagine you're playing the piano and you see a D note.
- A Flat sign ♭ means you have to move one step to the **left**, to the very next key which is a black key called Db

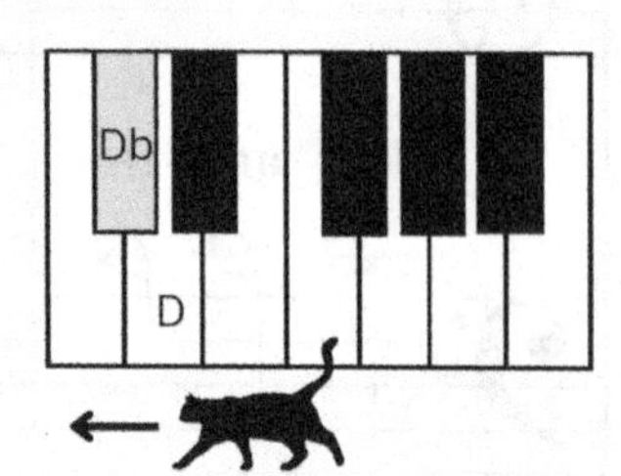

*C# is also the same note as Db.

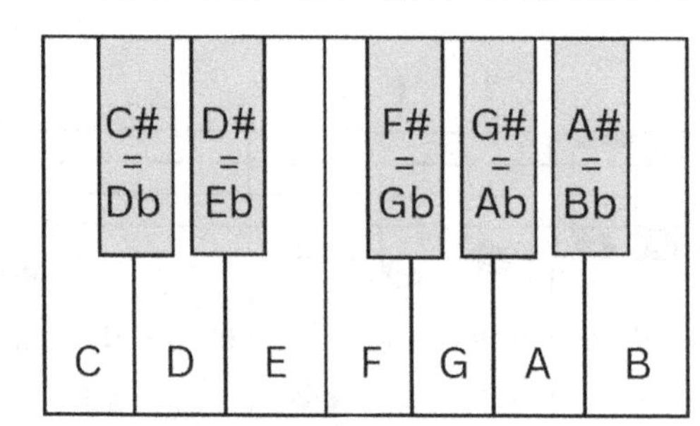

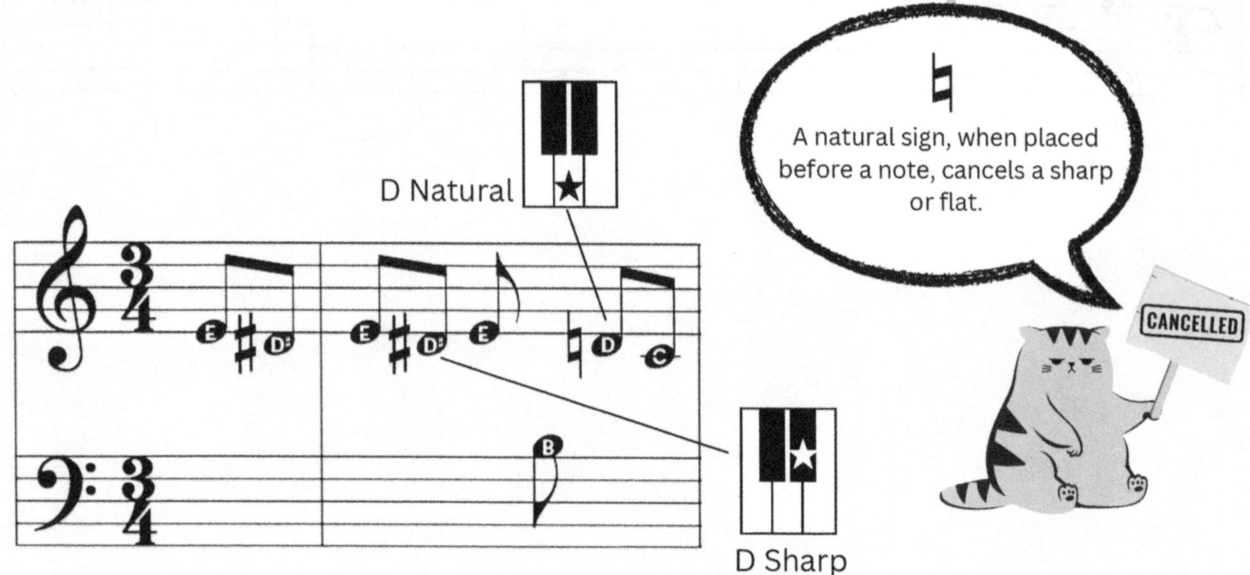

Practice drawing ♯, ♭ and ♮ by tracing over guidelines. Draw 2 more in the remaining space.

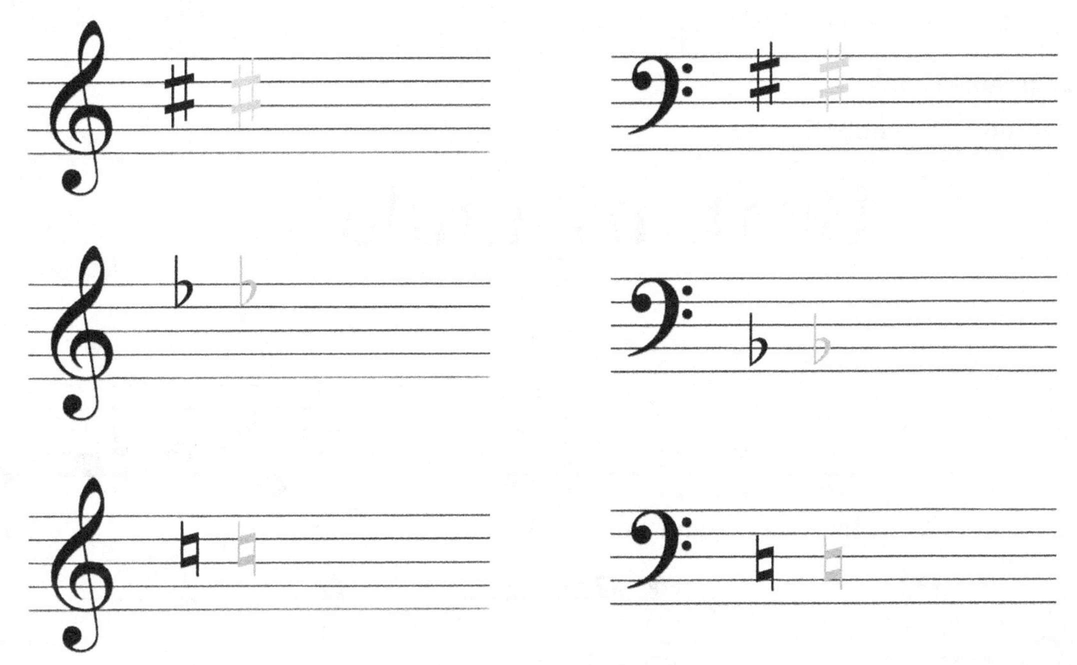

Draw a line from the key with the star on the keyboard to the 2 correct note names - one flat and one sharp. The first one is done for you.

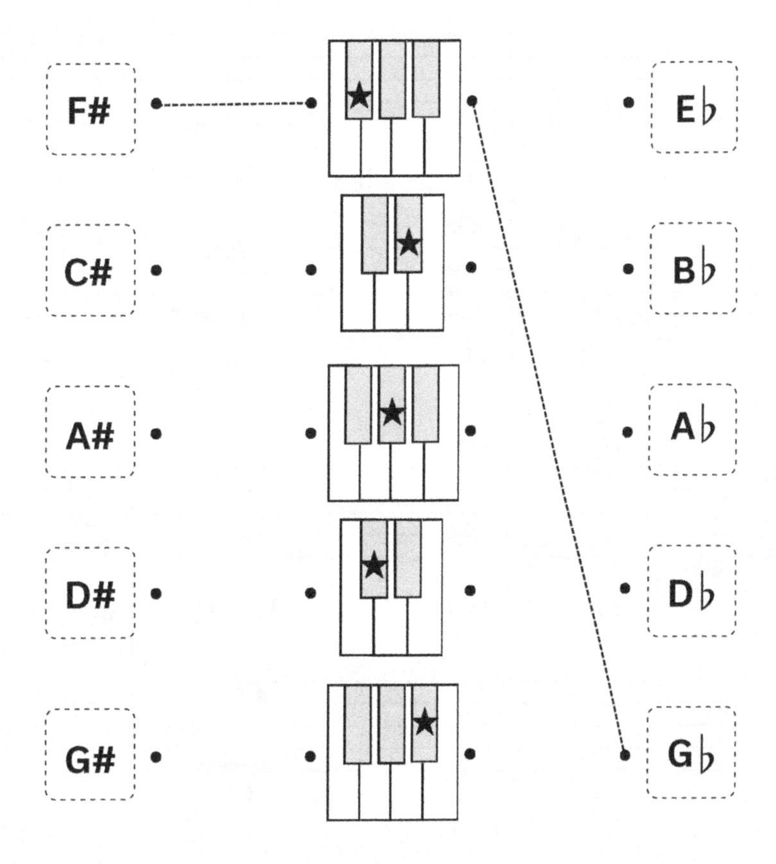

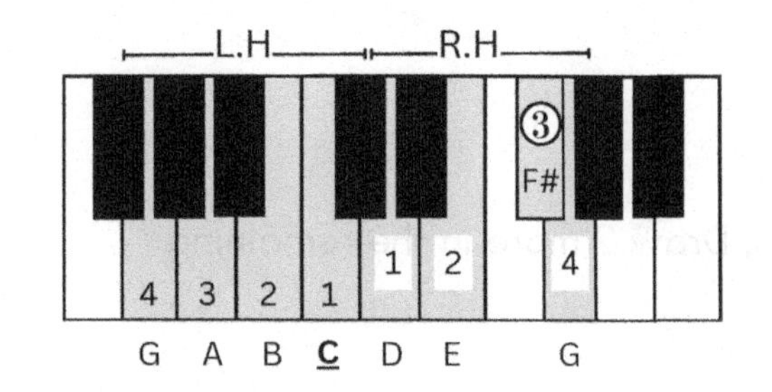

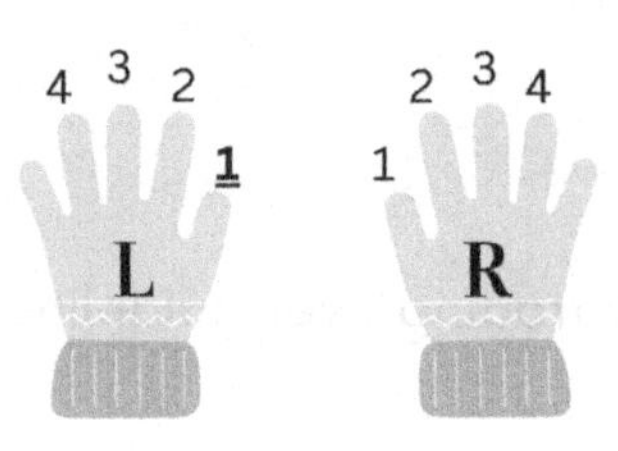

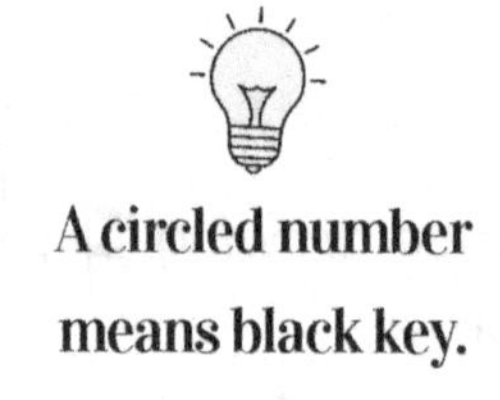

A circled number means black key.

Right hand thumb on D
Left hand thumb on middle C

Brahms' Lullaby

Johannes Brahms

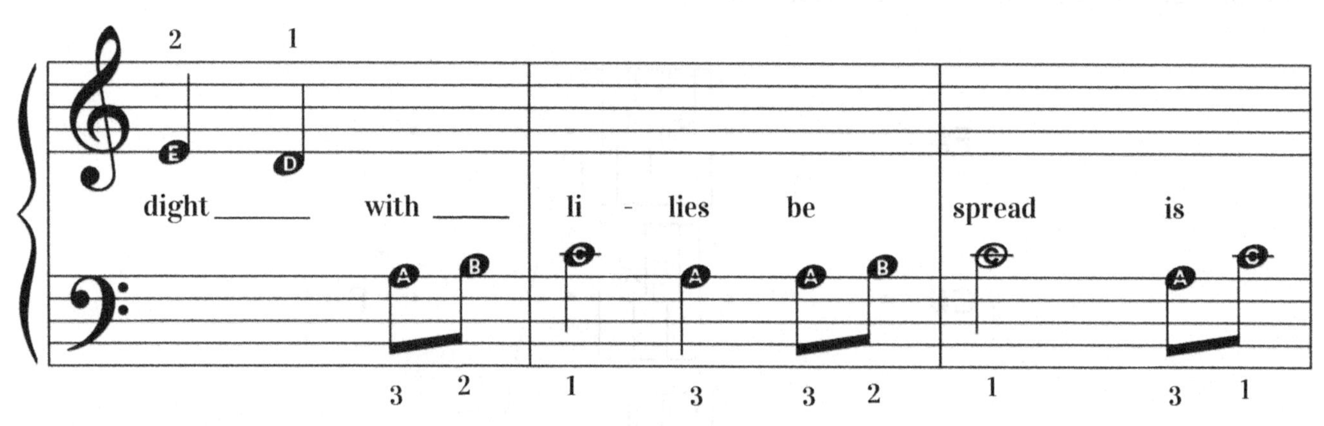

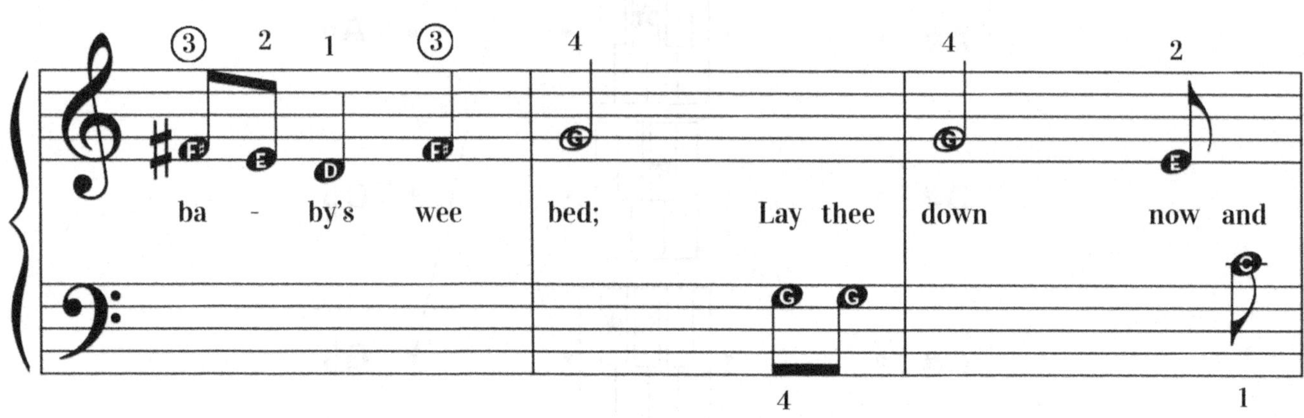

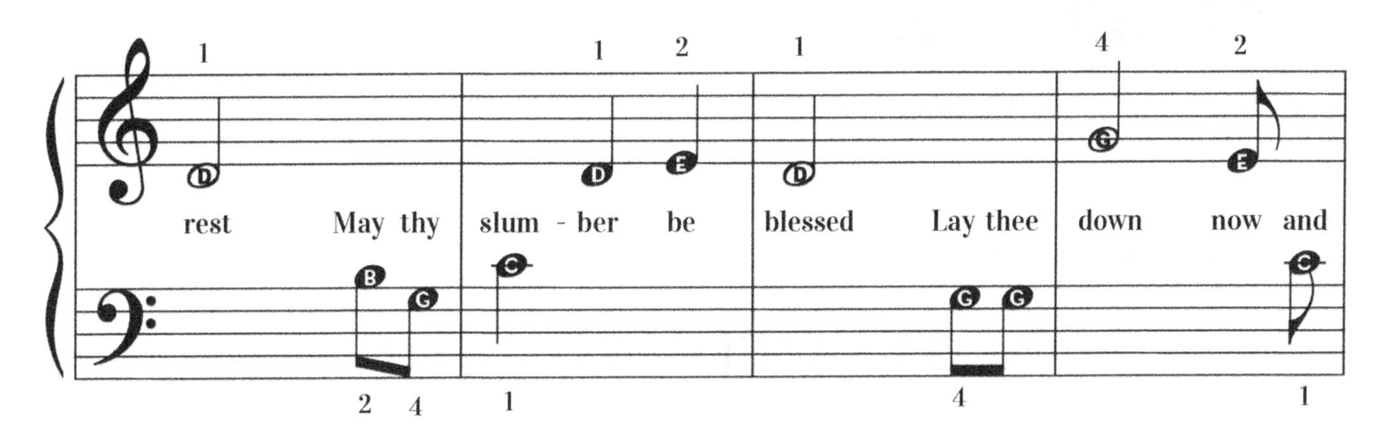
1
1 2
1
4 2
rest May thy slum - ber be blessed Lay thee down now and
2 4 1
4
1

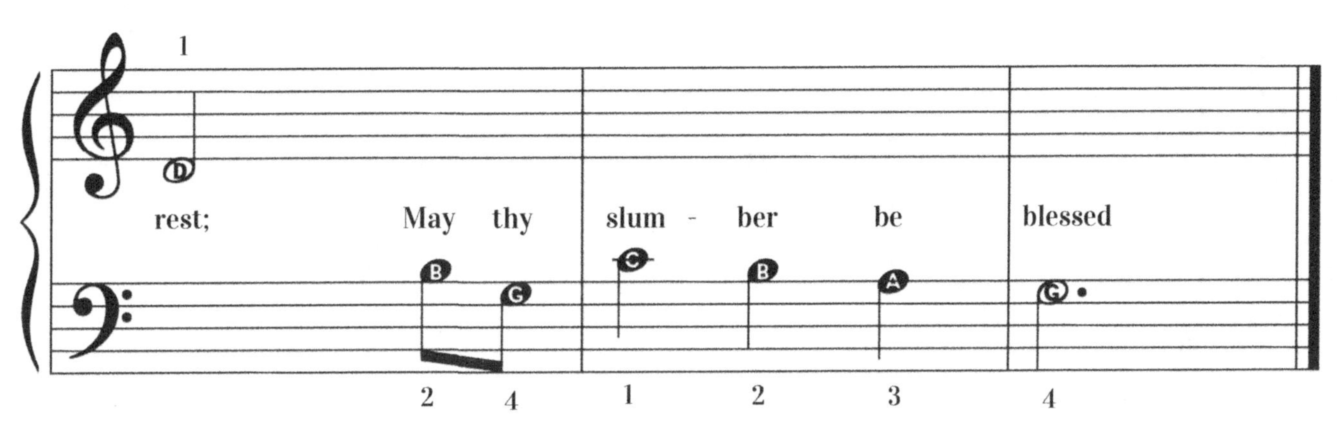
1
rest; May thy slum - ber be blessed
2 4 1 2 3 4

Why is crossing the street like playing the piano?
You need to C# or you might Bb!

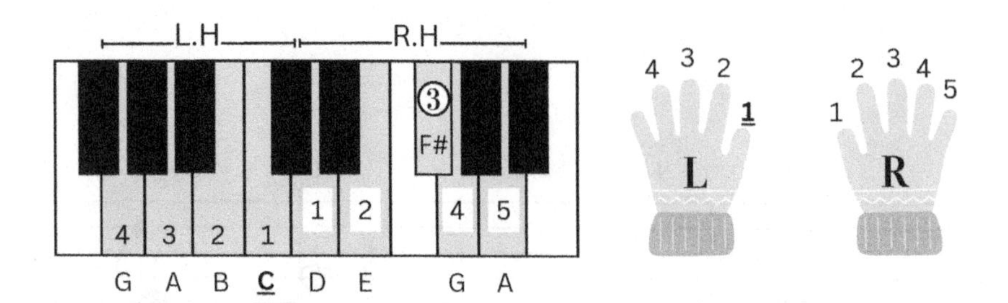

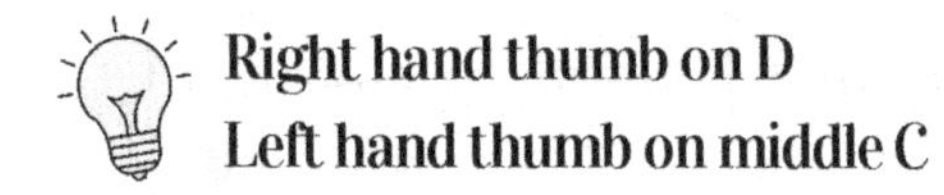

Scarborough Fair

Traditional

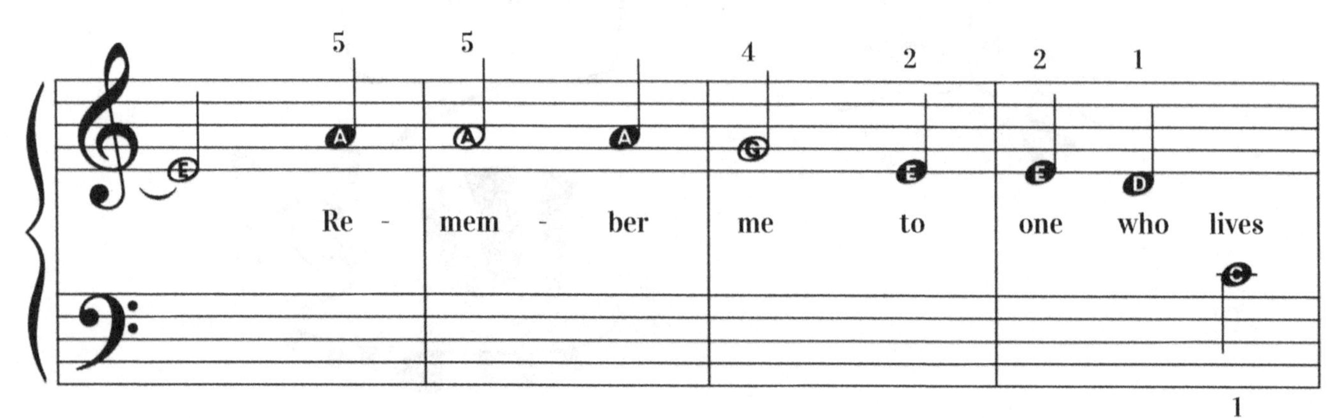

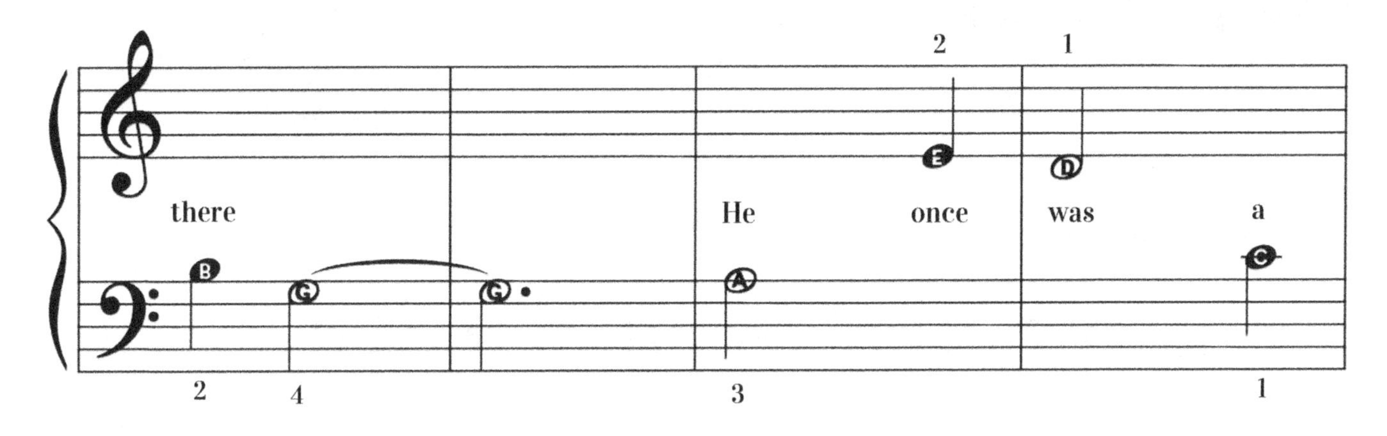
2 1
E D
there He once was a
B G G A C
2 4 3 1

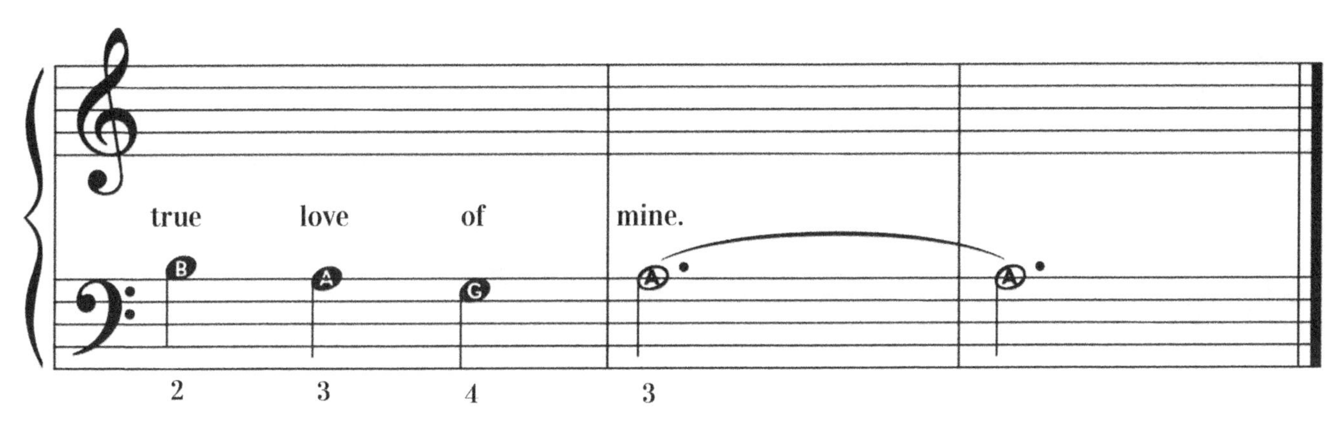
true love of mine.
B A G A A
2 3 4 3

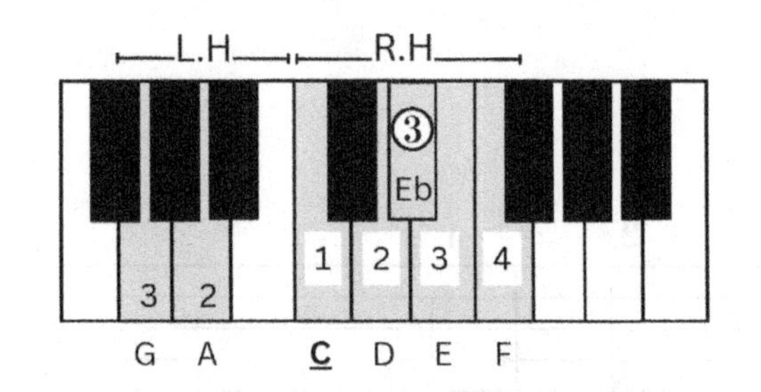

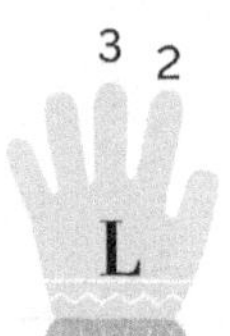

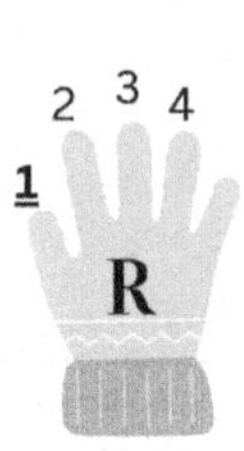

Right hand thumb on middle C
Left hand thumb on B

A Sailor Went To Sea

Traditional

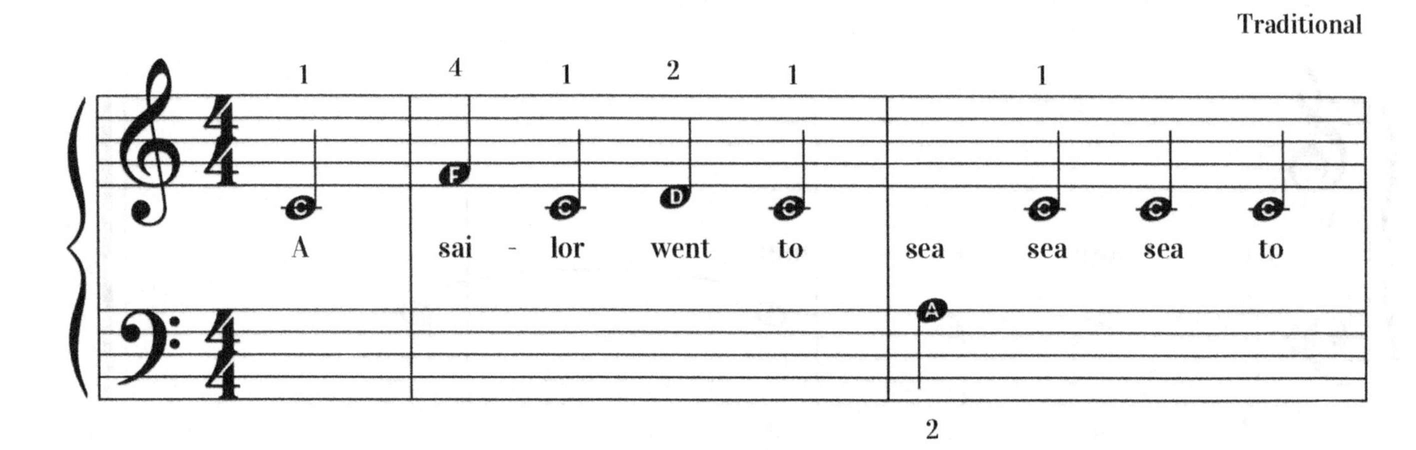

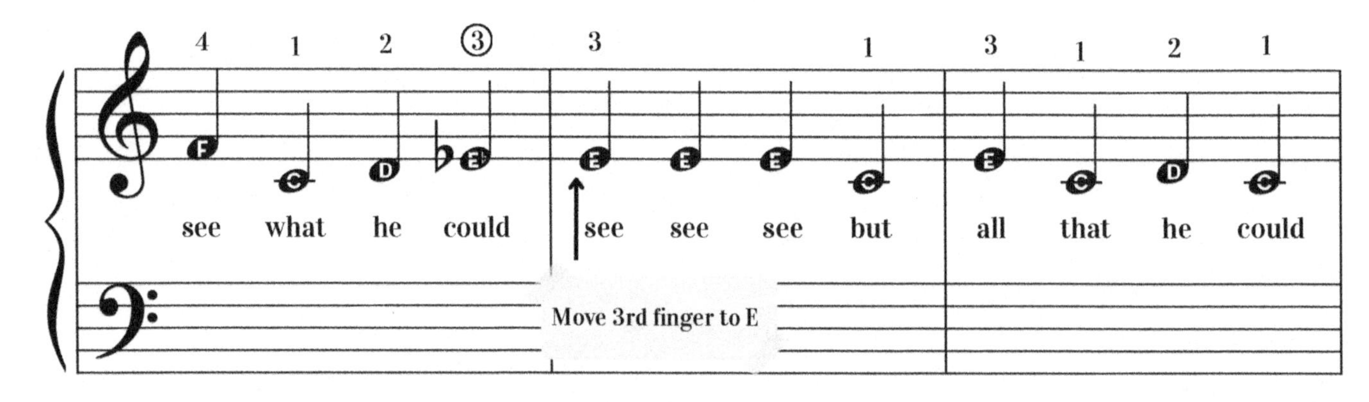

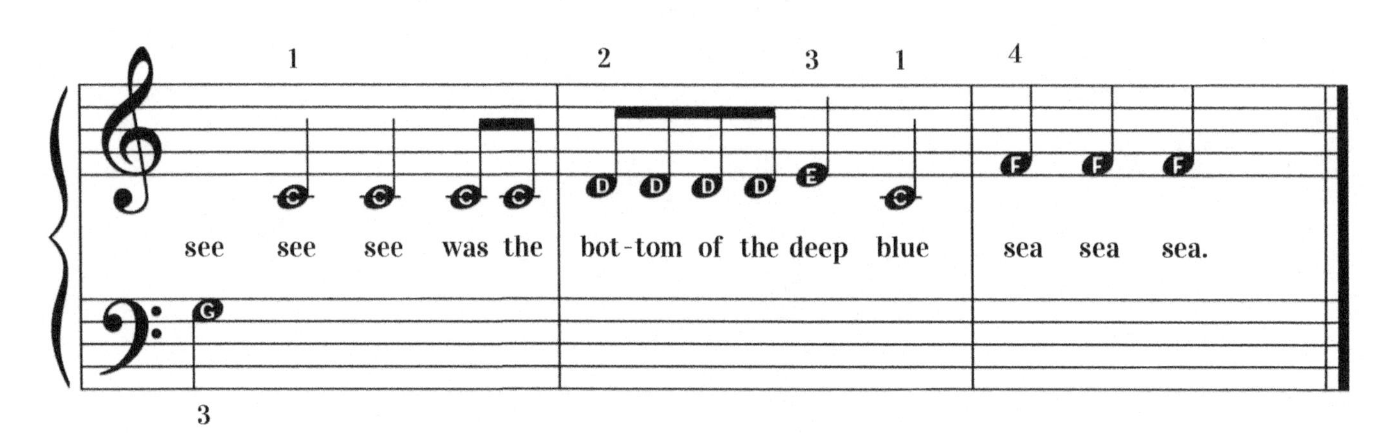

Bonus Song

LET'S PLAY FÜR ELISE

Who is Beethoven?

Ludwig van Beethoven was an incredible musician born over 250 years ago. He started playing music when he was very young and became one of the most famous composers ever. Beethoven wrote many beautiful pieces, including "Für Elise," that people still love to play and listen to today.

What's "Für Elise" Mean?

"Für Elise" is German, and it means "For Elise" in English. But guess what? Nobody knows exactly who Elise was! Some think it might have been Beethoven's friend or someone he liked a lot.

A Lost Treasure!

Did you know "Für Elise" was hidden for 40 years after Beethoven wrote it? A music teacher named Ludwig Nohl found it and shared it with the world. Now, it's a favorite tune for piano players everywhere!

Do you know that I, Beethoven, started losing my hearing in my late 20s? But I kept composing music anyway. I wrote my Ninth Symphony when I was almost deaf.

Wow Impressive, I'm glad you never gave up! We could all use a bit of your dedication especially when I need my dinner served!

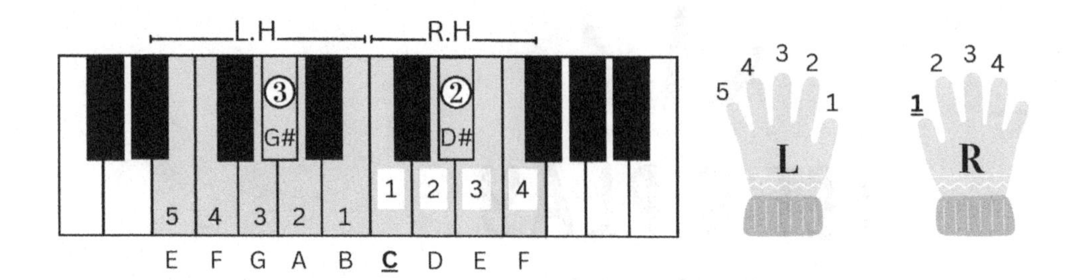

Right hand thumb on middle C
Left hand thumb on B

Für Elise

Ludwig van Beethoven

Music Practice BINGO

Try out these practice ideas next time you play!

Tap the rhythm of the song. Tap Left hand for left hand parts, right hand for right hand parts	Play the song in slow "turtle" speed	Playing while singing	Memorize the whole song
Play loud!	Repeat a small section of the song that you found challenging	Play the whole song with no mistake	Play super soft..
Recite the lyrics with the correct rhythm	Play the entire song while only looking at the music sheet	Play two bars of music with your eyes closed	Tap your feet to count the beat while playing
Practice for 30 minutes	Say the letter name while playing	Play it for a friend, family member or pet!	Play the song in a different octave

Answer Key

Chapter 1

1,5
4,1
2,3,2,4

C, E, C, F
D, F, G, E
F, D, E, F

C, E, F
D, C, G
G, E, D

5, 2, 4, 3, 6

Chapter 2

A, E, B, A
B, F, G, E
F, D, C, G

C, E, F, G
D, G, G, A
F, C, E, B

Chapter 3

G
D
F
E
A

A
F
B
G
C

Chapter 4

F#
C#
A#
D#
G#

E♭
B♭
A♭
D♭
G♭

Top Secret p.22

1143
1122
4123
3124
3134

Top Secret p.57

cafe
face
cage
bag
bead

Top Secret p.59

Bb	E	C	A#	G	C#	D
C	C	D	Eb	G	C	C
F	A	G	B	F	D	F
Bb	B	Gb	F	A	A	E
A	G	A	B	D	E	A
G	C	D#	C	A	C#	B
D	D	G	B	A	G	F

Top Secret p.27

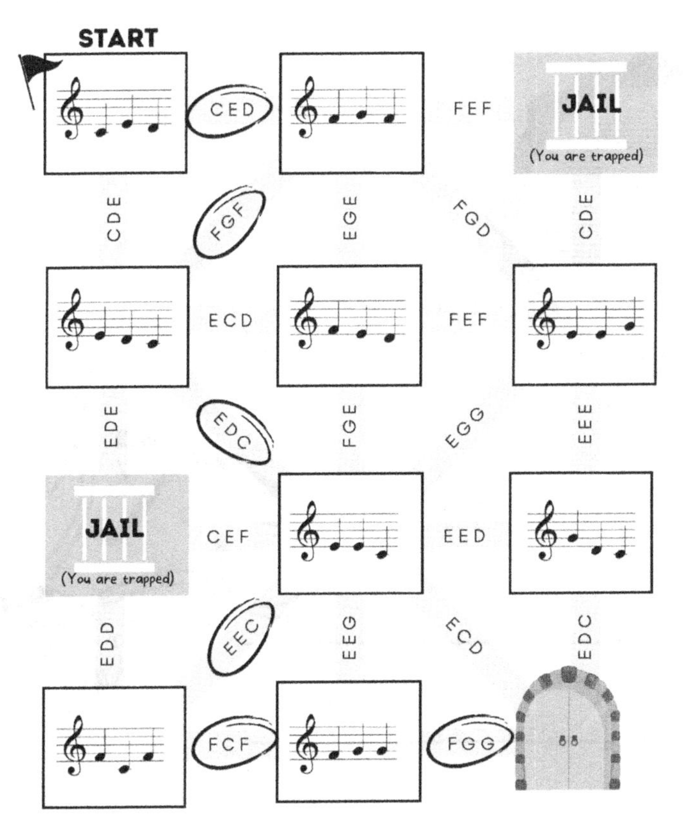

CERTIFICATE

OF ACHIEVEMENT

PROUDLY PRESENTED TO:

____

Congratulations on completing this book! Your dedication and hard work have paid off.

Date Completed: ____________________

Teacher: ____________________

Reference + DIY Keyboard Label

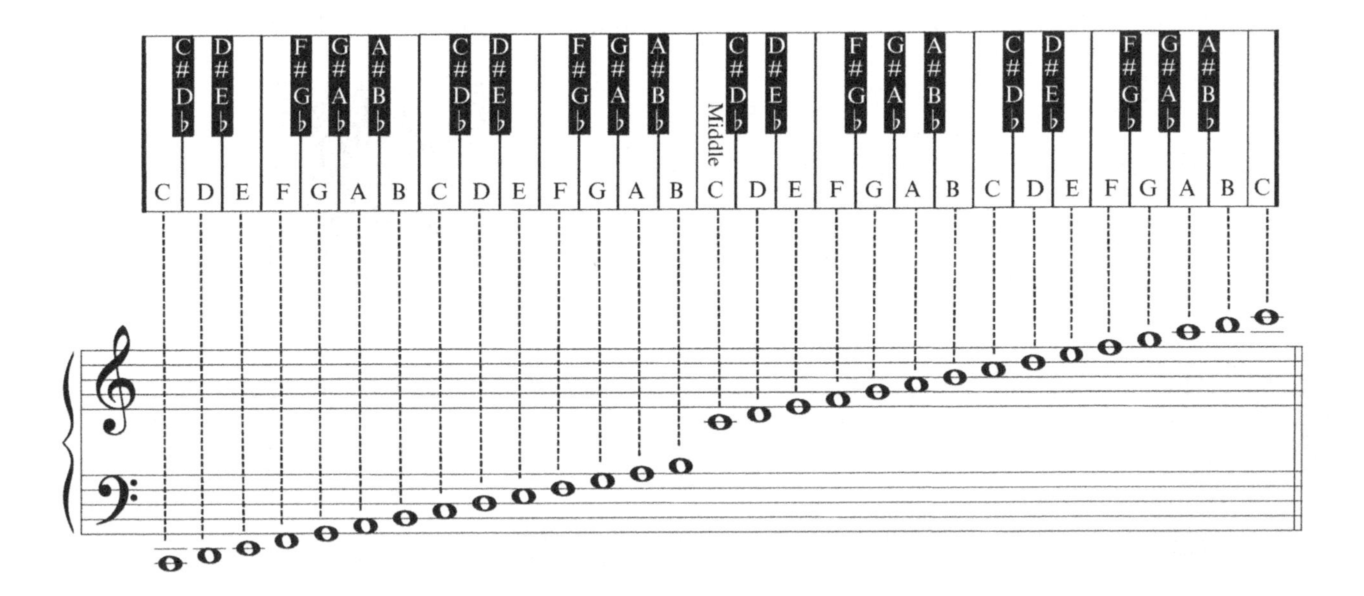

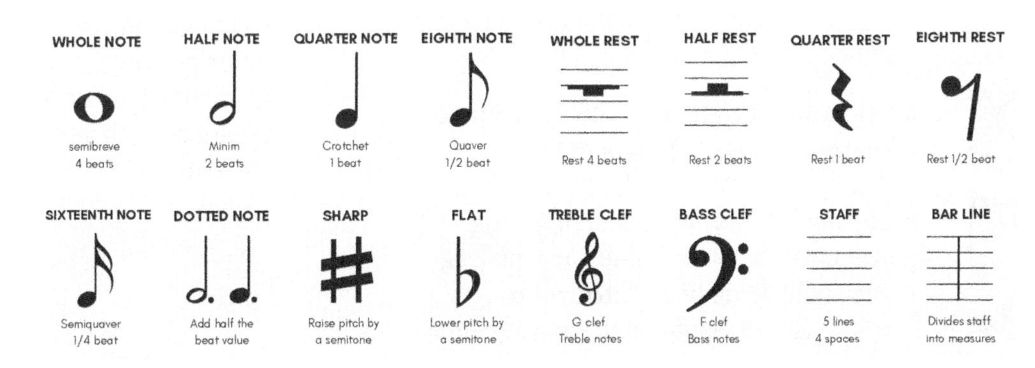

Cut out this square and tape it on your keyboard for quick note location.

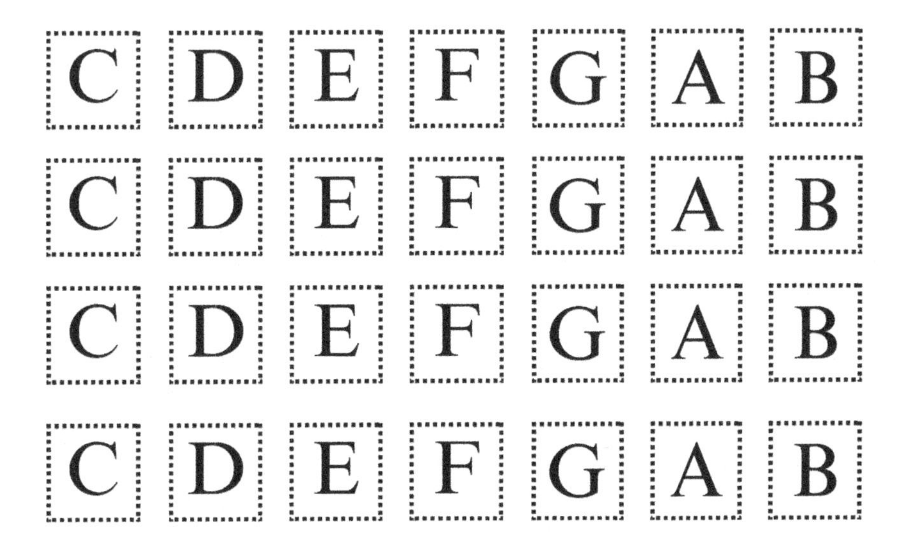

Share Your Musical Journey: Review us on Amazon!

Thank you for reaching this point in the book! I thoroughly enjoyed writing it and sincerely hope you found it beneficial. I would be truly grateful for your feedback on your experience. Your candid insights are important in helping me improve my future content and create the best resources possible for musicians. If you have any private feedback or question, you can send it to lidomusicpublishing@outlook.com

Thank you!

Explore More Music Books by Lido Publishing

If you've enjoyed this Children's songbook, you might find our other beginner friendly piano books helpful. Scan this QR code to discover more titles from the same author.

Scales Chords Arpeggios

"From beginner to advanced levels. With over 600 entries in all Major and Minor Keys - fully illustrated with three levels - fingerings, visual guides, chord charts and more!"

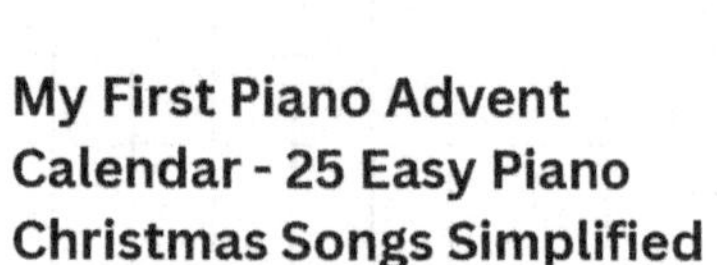

My First Piano Advent Calendar - 25 Easy Piano Christmas Songs Simplified

"Designed for anyone who can't read music yet, this book uses simplified notation. With large note heads, letter names and clear instructions. Includes lyrics, guitar chords, visual hand position chart and a daily countdown to Christmas."

Music Advent Calendar - 25 Easy Piano Christmas Songs (2 levels in 1)

"25 easy Christmas carols for beginners, featuring two levels, lyrics, fingering, guitar chords, letter names and no page turns. Include daily countdown to Christmas and visual hand position chart"